A wonderfully rich resource for anyone wanting practical help with guilt issues. Van der Hart and Waller chart a wise course between unbalanced extremes. They integrate the best of professional psychological wisdom with classic, orthodox Christian theology. Some hard truths and a timely message to the church.
Dr Crispin Fletcher-Louis, theologian and previously Principal of Westminster Theological Centre

Will van der Hart and Rob Waller have forged a formidable alliance between pastor and psychiatrist to author an original and mind-changing book. Anchored in the teaching of the Bible and faithfully shaped by it, *The Guilt Book* integrates wide-ranging insights from modern psychology, as well as the authors' extensive clinical and pastoral experience. Distinguishing between true guilt and the many disguises of false guilt, they succeed in making the complex simple, whilst never being simplistic. Their counsel is biblical, intellectually rigorous and intensely practical. Read this book quickly. And then read it again, slowly and reflectively. You will be challenged, provoked, and quite possibly liberated by its wise counsel.
Professor Glynn Harrison, Emeritus Professor of Psychiatry, University of Bristol

As I read this book, I could feel the hold of some of my false guilt beginning to dissolve. It dissolved in the warmth of this book's compassion, and in the light of its truth, both biblical and psychological. I could feel new health growing in my mind. This is a map to a better place, a place of inner freedom.
Revd Shaun Lambert, Senior Minister of Stanmore Baptist Church and author of A Book of Sparks: A Study in Christian Mind*Full*ness

The hearts of the a   ent to equip
the reader to reach   ic
viewpoint, includin   and a biblical

D1439961

grounding. An accessible read about true and false guilt and the first steps to a complete solution for a corrosive problem.

Kay Lawrence, Harley Street Humanistic-Integrative Counsellor, London

Guilt gets you stuck in life . . . I know. When you get stuck, you need help. This book will offer you that help. It has the capacity to free you to live life in all its fullness. Some books are highly readable but not much use. Other books are really useful but dull as dishwater. Rob and Will have written a book you will want to read, and which will help you become the person you want to be.

Revd Karl Martin, Senior Pastor, Central, Edinburgh

Here's a great resource that is well based in the Bible and contemporary counselling practice and yet is practical, manageable, and provides a step-by-step guide towards being set free from guilt, as Christ intends.

Derek Tidball, former Principal of London School of Theology

Guilt is something I have always been weighed down by, and I know so many friends who have the same battle, reliving situation after situation in our heads. This book looks both theologically and practically at helping me see where my thinking has gone wonky and enabling me to realize it doesn't have to be that way. Can't really recommend this book highly enough! I will be returning to it over and over.

Katharine Welby, writer and blogger

The Guilt Book

To those who struggle with guilt

ivp

The Guilt Book

A path to grace and freedom

Will van der Hart
& Rob Waller

INTER-VARSITY PRESS
36 Causton Street, London SW1P 4ST, England
Email: ivp@ivpbooks.com
Website: www.ivpbooks.com

First published 2014
Reprinted 2017

British Library Cataloguing-in-Publication Data
A catalogue record for this book is available from the British Library.

ISBN: 978-1-78359-116-9
eBook ISBN: 978-1-78359-117-6

Set in Dante 12/15pt

Typeset in Great Britain by CRB Associates, Potterhanworth, Lincolnshire
Printed and bound in Great Britain by Ashford Colour Press Ltd, Gosport, Hampshire

Inter-Varsity Press publishes Christian books that are true to the Bible and that communicate the gospel, develop discipleship and strengthen the church for its mission in the world.

IVP originated within the Inter-Varsity Fellowship, now the Universities and Colleges Christian Fellowship, a student movement connecting Christian Unions in universities and colleges throughout Great Britain, and a member movement of the International Fellowship of Evangelical Students. Website: www.uccf.org.uk. That historic association is maintained, and all senior IVP staff and committee members subscribe to the UCCF Basis of Faith.

Contents

Acknowledgments

Rob would like to thank the NHS for its continued support throughout his employment and training, and Will thanks his colleagues and friends in the diocese of London, particularly The Rt Revd and Rt Hon. Bishop Richard Chartres who has been such an inspiration in his ministry. We are both grateful to the editorial and marketing team at IVP (particularly Eleanor Trotter) for their skill and patience in working with our many drafts, and also for sharing our vision for this book. We would also like to thank those who have written commendations, J.John for his Foreword and Charlie Mackesy for his artwork.

We are both indebted to our wives, Susanna and Lucinda, and to our families, far more than we can say, and of course to our God, who has taught us much about guilt, love, forgiveness and the hope we share.

Foreword

A key Christian belief is that human beings are seriously messed up. And in no area of life is our mess greater than in the area of guilt. (You might argue that sex should have that dubious honour, but where would sexual sin be without guilt?)

It is easy to forget that guilt can be a good thing. What we might call good guilt is the warning icon on the dashboard of life that points out precisely what has failed and where. Good guilt inflicts a clean wound: the pure surgical sting of the certainty in our conscience that we have done wrong and need God's forgiveness for some specific act, word or thought. Good guilt is sharply focused and points us Godward. When we bring whatever caused it before the Father who loves us, the Son who redeems us and the Holy Spirit who restores us, the wounds of good guilt heal rapidly and leave few traces. Good guilt brings with it both purpose and the potential for healing. It guides us to the cross of Christ and to the blessed lands of fellowship with God beyond.

Yet, for every ounce of good guilt around, there is a ton of the bad stuff, the diabolical counterfeit and destroyer of lives:

false guilt. False guilt is the nagging, haunting remorse for something that was either not a sin at all or a matter so trivial that everybody else has long since forgotten it. False guilt is widespread; indeed, it may almost be universal. Ask any pastor, any psychiatrist or quite simply anybody who has seriously looked at their life. In reality, you probably don't need me to tell you how widespread and damaging it is. False guilt is a whisperer: it tells us that we have failed, brings to our attention every flaw in our existence and undermines any sense of worth. False guilt is a poisoner: it creates septic wounds that infect souls and lives. False guilt is a mocker: it sneers at all our achievements, ridicules our hopes of grace and denies our every attempt to do good.

Guilt – and how to deal with it – is the subject of this excellent book. In introducing it, let me point out several specific features that strike me about the false variety.

The first feature of false guilt is how often it involves a general and unfocused accusation. I am sure we have all heard that little voice: 'you've blown it again' and 'you really aren't a very good person, are you?' The accusations are always non-specific, always hurtful and they never direct us to a God of grace who longs to forgive. Not for nothing is the devil described in the Bible as 'the accuser of our brothers and sisters, who accuses them before our God day and night . . .' (Revelation 12:10). It is hardly surprising that false guilt is non-specific. After all, if it focused on something in particular, we could repent of it.

A second feature of false guilt is that it is not a single, simple evil of the mind; it is a general malaise that allows other ills to attack us. False guilt (and even unforgiven good guilt) can easily be misused against us or – God forbid – by us. How many children have been made to feel guilty over the failure of their parents' marriages? How many spouses have been made to believe by their partners that they, and they alone, are responsible for this or that unhappiness? Guilt can be manipulated. To make someone feel guilty about something is to be halfway to controlling them.

A third harmful feature of false guilt is that it misleads. One of the curiosities of false guilt is that we know it is phoney. Even as we feel haunted about some decades-old trivial misunderstanding, we know that the guilt we feel is ridiculous. Yet here is the real danger: false guilt brings good guilt into disrepute. We can easily fall into the trap of thinking that all sense of blame is equally worthless, and in so doing throw out the baby of true guilt with the bathwater of the false. This is a disaster, because to despise true guilt is to tear down the bridge that leads to God.

A final and tragic feature of false guilt is the way that it endures. There are far too many men and women of advanced age who have long forgotten the decent things they did half a century ago but can remember with unerring accuracy the trivial things they did wrong. Or, to be more precise, what they *think* they did wrong: false guilt is, after all, an utter liar. The long-term persistence of false guilt is hardly surprising; it is exactly because it is false that it is hard to deal with. After all, how can you repent and receive forgiveness when, at the heart of the problem, there may be nothing to repent and receive forgiveness for?

It is for this and other reasons that false guilt needs exposing. I am very grateful for this thoughtful and insightful book. Yet this is more than simply an *Observer's Guide to False Guilt* which does no more than catalogue the types of false guilt. This is a book written by that fertile combination of a pastor and a psychiatrist. Theology and psychology have long been seen as enemies, but it is precisely in areas like this that the two subjects can be brought together with enormously beneficial results.

With pastoral sensitivity and wisdom, the authors offer the reader an opportunity to identify and purge false guilt.

It is my hope and prayer that this book will liberate many from guilt they thought they could never be rid of, so that God can bless them in ways they could never imagine.

J.John (Revd Canon)
www.philotrust.com

Introduction

*There's no problem so awful that you can't add
some guilt to it and make it even worse.*
Calvin: in *Calvin and Hobbes,* by Bill Watterson

Guilt is underrated. People undervalue its benefits in spiritual diagnosis and guidance. It is also underrated in its subtle ability to disable, distract and destroy.

True guilt is a blessing from God. Without it we would feel no remorse, seek no forgiveness and find no restoration. True guilt is what leads us to the One who can 'forgive us our sins, for we also forgive everyone who sins against us' (Luke 11:4). Far from being a burden that we should analyse or avoid, true guilt is something we should be thankful for and listen to.

Yet most people, including many Christians, suffer from the torment of distorted guilt, something we shall call 'false guilt' in the pages of this book. Far from being a positive influence in our lives, this robs us of the 'good news' of the gospel.[1] Through the lens of false guilt, the spiritual realities of forgiveness, debts paid and a restored relationship with God are seen as ineffective.

False guilt is seen in unhappiness, anxiety and indecision. It can cause compulsive caring, a rebound into rebellion or a bitter refusal to enjoy life. At its worst, false guilt can be the cause of depression and even suicidal thoughts. Sixteenth-century theologian and pastor John Calvin responded to the problem of false guilt by saying, 'The torture of a bad conscience is the hell of a living soul.'

This is a common problem. Whether you have just happened upon this book, or are reading it on the recom-mendation of a friend, we want you to know that you are in good company. Struggles with guilt have been an ongoing experience of believers past and present who have been both convinced of the power of the gospel and yet still plagued by heavy guilt.

A personal journey

Both Rob and I (Will) struggle with the distortions of false guilt in different ways, and you will read detailed reflections from us in the course of the following chapters. Significant components of the anxiety disorder I suffer from are doubt and guilt. Diagnosis was a huge blessing to me, as I could then see that not all my thoughts and feelings were to be believed as fact. Rob is more your typical overachiever, suppressing both true and false guilt in the name of progress. It took him some years to realize that there is such a thing as having done 'enough' – and he is still learning how to rest. Many similar stories and reflections from others will illustrate this book.

I remember a key turning point in my struggle with guilt. While praying many years ago, I had an image of a man in a prison cell. The door had been thrown open, and light streamed through the window. Jesus was calling the man out, and yet he would not move because he felt too guilty.

I have returned to this picture many times in the course of my ministry, as I have encountered scores of people like me who, despite being set free by Christ, remained prisoners of guilt. Very rarely have I ever found any correlation between the gravity of their actual sins and the state of their crippled consciences! Indeed, it would seem that those who struggle with guilt the most are often those who have the least to feel guilty about. Of course, typically, they themselves would not believe this to be the case.

How this book works
The purpose of this book is to take the reader on a personal journey of just a few yards: the journey across the prison cell and out through the open door. This may sound like a

simple undertaking, but it is a challenging reality and will take courage and commitment from any reader who really struggles with false guilt. Typically, we take another kind of journey called a 'guilt trip', which nails us firmly to the opposite wall, as we accuse and berate ourselves into inactivity.

To ensure the greatest level of success in achieving this task, Rob and I will lead you through a considered blend of information, theology, psychology and activity. Paul Tournier, Swiss psychotherapist and theologian, closes his book *Guilt and Grace* by saying, 'Guilt is . . . a religious problem which interests theologians, a social problem which interests sociologists and a psychological problem which interests psychologists.'[2] All these disciplines have a helpful perspective, and in this book we will show how each offers some helpful tools.

Our starting point is the Bible and what it tells us about right and wrong – for that is where guilt has to be evaluated as either true or false. However, in dealing with false guilt, we will draw on the huge amount that has been learnt about the human mind by psychologists and psychiatrists over the last few decades. We have found that their 'how' to change works in harmony with the faith-based 'why' to change.

Psychology, like medicine, is not normally contrary to Christianity – instead, these two disciplines will often bring different yet complementary approaches to particular parts of the problem. We can understand the true salvation landscape we will journey through, but also how it can become distorted by man-made views.

We will also be asking you to take notes and do some exercises, which may at times be testing. There are no tricks or shortcuts. It will do you no good just to read this book. You might pick up a few nuggets of useful information, but these will do little to reduce your suffering unless followed by decisive action. Your application to these tasks and your determination to endure some painful emotions are the best way to support your own recovery.

Who this book is for

This book is primarily for Christians who struggle with guilt. You may have a recurrent worry about something you did many years ago that you cannot shake off. You might be regularly plagued by guilt over all manner of things. You might be reading this book with a view to helping someone else. All of these are good reasons to try to understand guilt better. There will be some people who also need professional help, and we will offer some guidance on this in Appendix 2 (page 180).

If you don't have a personal faith in Jesus, please continue to read this book, as it is highly relevant for you too. The first thing to make clear is that the psychological principles that we outline will be of benefit to you in their own right. If you engage with the exercises, you will, we believe, gain significant clarity and relief from false guilt. Equally, within these pages you will also get an exciting insight into the remedy for true guilt that is at the very heart of the Christian message. Should you wish it, this is something you can also receive for yourself.

Rob and I have our work cut out. Some of the people we have written this book for will have felt guilty about buying it! Others will struggle to take any approach other than what they consider a purely 'spiritual' one, for fear of offending God. Most will be repressing a large amount of the guilt they feel. But our readers are the ones who have made a start on their journey, for the really guilty may not read it at all. So, if you have come this far, well done!

Making your journey to freedom

Before setting out on this journey to greater freedom, you will need to do a bit of planning. For your map, you will find below an overview of the book. For your companions, we remind you that you should not go it alone. And all good navigators know that to use your map, you first need accurately to determine your starting point, so let's take a snapshot of 'now'.

Your map

The early chapters of *The Guilt Book* are filled with fact-finding, information and testimony. The reason for including these is to help create a clear perspective on the problem and strengthen your own ability to distinguish between true and false guilt.

The greatest risk of you sabotaging your recovery from guilt comes from the fear that you may mistake something that is 'true' for something that is 'false' – often those with a Christian faith are particularly concerned about this. We will introduce these two types of guilt, and the more confident you are in identifying them, the more successful you will be in dealing appropriately with both. It might be helpful to think of guilt as both a condition (whether or not you have done something wrong) and an emotion (a feeling that may or may not reflect what you have actually done).

We will spend a whole chapter covering how the good news of the Christian gospel deals with true guilt. And although this may be material you have heard before, it is worth a read to review it and see if it has been wrongly applied to false guilt or been ineffective where it was in fact needed.

We will look at what keeps guilt going, as we believe it to be an *active* process rather than simply the result of not having asked for forgiveness or having continued to sin. We will look at the brain pathways involved, and also the relationships between guilt and mental illness when things can really become entrenched and professional help can be needed. Rob, as a consultant psychiatrist, and I myself, as a church minister with considerable psychological understanding, want you to feel safe and comfortable with the insights and tools we suggest. We will be clear when we think you need to hear a spiritual perspective first, and also when you need to be talking to a doctor or counsellor. We will also look at culture and how it can involve guilt as a motivator, and our churches which can do this too.

We will then teach you a series of techniques to help with the short-lived spikes of guilt and the more long-term shame. Some things can be fully fixed; you will need to learn to live alongside others – but both approaches can be seen as recovery. Lastly, we will introduce you to the partnership between true guilt and true joy, which will guide us in our onward journey towards the One who has called us to live guilt-free.

Your mates

Friends can be a great help on this journey. Guilt is usually a very private thing, but secrecy is one of the things that can prolong guilt. You have probably had *acquaintances* tell you that such and such is nothing to feel guilty about – yet this is ineffective for change. You have probably offered this view to others, but cannot apply it to yourself. However, one or two *good friends* who say this and still want to know you and love you can speak more effectively than words. You can read the book with them or just touch base every now and again.

God is the best journeyman of all, even if you feel far from him. He is the sinner's friend, even if you do not feel his forgiveness yet. He actually said that he 'did not come to judge the world, but to save the world' (John 12:47). Perhaps you can still spend time with him and let him bear some of the burden as you travel. We would ask you to seek his help to engage fully in the journey marked out here. We would also advise against the temptation to use superficial prayers, such as 'God, take it all away', for this can be a way of avoiding the hard work that must be done.

Your mug-shot

When guilty criminals are sent to prison, they have their pictures taken. Typically, these show someone looking glum, condemned and sometimes remorseful. Think about an emotionally honest 'mug-shot' of yourself right now. What would it look like? Try to capture the reality of your struggle with guilt beyond the smiles and façades that you may be showing the people around you. Taking a reality check at the start of this journey will help you later as you track your progress and celebrate your victories.

Your destination – the haven of peace

Enid Blyton, in her book *The Folk of the Faraway Tree*,[3] tells a story: 'There was a tiny goblin who had once done a wicked thing, and couldn't forget it. He wanted to know the secret of forgetting, and that is one of the most difficult secrets in the world if you have done something really bad.' As I (Will) read this to my children, it passed over their heads, but I felt a tinge of sadness that forgetting should be a recommended way of solving the problem.

Forgetting like this is the proverbial ostrich putting its head into the sand – when the real world continues all around us. Yet, it appears to be the primary means by which people believe they will be able to leave their guilt behind. Jim

Carrey's film *Eternal Sunshine of the Spotless Mind* shows how unworkable this technique really is.[4] At best, it is a short-term fix, and the problem will just bubble up later, not to mention the added complications that arise because something is hidden away.

The destination of our journey is not 'The Secret of Forgetting'. Instead, it is 'The Place of Honest Remembering'. Our work is to embrace God's work of redemption and to live in its presence, neither underestimating nor exaggerating those things in us for which Christ had to die. As Charles Spurgeon said, 'Great thoughts of your sin alone will drive you to despair; but great thoughts of Christ will pilot you into the haven of peace.'[5] Once we have accurately remembered, then we can be forgiven and helpfully put things away – and start to find this peace.

Spend some time thinking about where you stand with guilt:

- What is the first thing that springs into your mind when you hear the word 'guilt'?

  _____

  _____

  _____

- How far does the expression 'Looking good, feeling bad' reflect your circumstances?

  _____

  _____

  _____

- What one thing would you want to be different in twelve months' time?

  _____

  _____

  _____

At the end of the book, we will invite you to take a 'welcome home' picture of yourself. We pray that there will be a significant difference: a picture of you breaking free – joy-filled, peaceful and feeling as light as a feather!

1. Guilty or not guilty – two types of guilt

Suspicion always haunts the guilty mind.
William Shakespeare: *Henry VI*, Part III

The guilty mind never rests, is never at peace and never quiet. It is suspicious even about its own conclusions. The resulting mistrust affects all of life: mistrust of God, mistrust of others and (here is the root) a mistrust of your own ability to know what is really going on. Guilty or not guilty? You simply cannot tell . . . Or this is what guilt would have you believe! A little perspective, however, can make a world of difference. Look at the story below. What might be going on? What can Mike do to feel better?

Mike had gone overdrawn. He was trying to get his mum's house redecorated, as she couldn't afford to do it herself. He borrowed money from a friend but he did not tell him the whole story, as he was too embarrassed about his family finances. Instead, he said he was a bit short at the end of the month and needed a loan – but then of course he could not pay it back.

He began a web of lies that destroyed their friendship. He felt guilty about the money, about his mum (even though she said that the house was now looking great) and about the loss of his friend.

In this simple story, we can see that Mike has indeed done some things wrong (he spent money he did not have, and then he lied). But he was also socially isolated (not able to be open with his friend at the start, and now he does not even have that friend). Additionally, he had some unhelpful beliefs (he predicted without evidence that his friend would not understand and he is guilty about his mum's house, despite having made a huge difference).

If you were his friend, you would long to say that it doesn't matter, that you understand, and maybe give him a hug or at least try to cheer him up! You might even help him see the different moral, social and mental components and take some steps towards tackling them in turn. Yet, Mike cannot apply this to himself – it all seems to blur, and his inner 'friend' tells him there is no way out of the mess.

Paul Tournier writes in *Guilt and Grace* that 'guilt cannot be dissected',[1] meaning that it is always complex and its causes are intertwined. But we don't agree: we think this can leave you stuck, as Mike is. Instead, we believe that even complex things *can* be broken down into bite-sized chunks. Some simple distinctions allow a fair degree of progress and even healing. Suspicion *can* always haunt the guilty mind, but there are some tools to test whether that suspicion is valid – and then show how to put it to bed.

Two types

Most books on guilt that we have read take a single approach to guilt, and so fall into the error of dealing with one type of guilt but not the other.

Some over-spiritualize guilt, giving a clear presentation of how the Christian gospel addresses sin, but failing to give enough consideration of the fact that most Christians who struggle with guilt are already forgiven in Jesus.

Others take an overly psychological approach. This in itself is neutral and not anti-Christian, but it does not tackle the root of sin. Also, in most secular texts, some lowering of moral standards is encouraged, or morals are not addressed at all. People feel falsely reassured.

The Christian faith encourages us to look at both the psychological and the spiritual. Psalm 139 ends with these verses:

Search me, God, and know my heart;
    test me and know my anxious thoughts.
See if there is any offensive way in me,
    and lead me in the way everlasting.
(Psalm 139:23–24)

It can be surprising to see such a well-loved psalm end with this focus on sin and soul searching. But if God is to know us right from our mother's womb (verse 13) and know all our days (verse 16), then surely he must know all our thoughts – including both the neurotic and the sinful. The interesting thing is that he does not seem to focus on one more than the other. He wants to help us with them both; he loves us just the same and he wants to 'know' us and 'lead' us throughout. He is the theological 'Saviour' and also the emotional 'Father' – addressing both our sin and our insecurity.

We therefore want to present two types of guilt. One type is the result of sin, which goes against God and creates a need that can be met only in Jesus. The other type is a distortion of reality – and needs a psychological answer. Respectively, we call these 'true guilt' and 'false guilt'.

Some definitions

Human conscience is our faculty for making moral judgments on the basis of our values and principles. It is influenced by genetic, social, familial and cultural factors. It can be proactive or reactive in relation to moral decisions.

Christian conscience is our conscience informed by the laws of God, the truth of the Bible and the presence of the Holy Spirit. It is far more *objective* than human conscience alone.

True guilt extends from a Christian conscience and, while it may be experienced as guilty feelings, it may simply be the acknowledgment of a negative moral state in which moral acts have been admitted and evaluated.

False guilt is typically experienced as persistent and distressing guilty feelings. False guilt can be present without any moral cause, but it generally amplifies, distorts or catastrophizes your worries or 'scruples', hence the term, 'a scrupulous conscience'.

Shame is a state of self-consciousness in which one's personhood is the focus of negative feelings (rather than guilt's moral actions). It often extends from false guilt, as unresolved 'bad acts' lead to the belief that one is inherently 'bad'. If you like, guilt is about the sin, and shame is about the sinner.

The importance of distinguishing between true and false guilt cannot be emphasized enough. The church is not paralysed by true guilt, but by false guilt. The church knows Jesus but still feels guilty; the Christian has repented but still feels trapped. The Bible also seems to make this distinction in 2 Corinthians 7:10, where it says, 'Godly sorrow brings repentance that leads to salvation and leaves no regret, but worldly sorrow brings death'.[2] Through identifying the false guilt, we can engage a different set of approaches that are effective and give hope to those who struggle in this way. The table overleaf draws some comparisons.

True guilt

One thing you can do if you are not sure if a particular thing would be seen as 'sinful' or not is to conduct a small survey of people you know who share your beliefs. You may be surprised at the responses, especially if you were being unhelpfully hard or lenient.

What a person considers to be behaviour worthy of what is 'true guilt' will depend considerably on their personal moral framework and the state of their human conscience. In this book, we will take a framework that comes from God and the Bible (the Christian conscience). Christians differ on some details, but there is general agreement on the cause and problems of sin. Christians believe that 'all have sinned and fall short of the glory of God' (Romans 3:23), and so all will feel a degree of true guilt because of this.

God also provides the only answers to true guilt: his forgiveness and a restored relationship. The Bible is full of stories of men and women who try to make their own sacrifices, who carry their own remorse and suffer vain regrets. However, forgiveness can only come when a price has been paid for the

True guilt	False guilt
Repentance brings forgiveness and peace	Repentance never feels like enough
Identity is gained; we are the forgiven children of God	Identity is lost; we do not feel worthy to be called his children
Lack of repentance is also called denial – we lack moral insight	Lack of repentance is not relevant, as there is nothing to repent of
Leads us towards God for forgiveness and salvation	Leads us away from God, believing the barrier to be insurmountable
Focuses on the root issue – our damaged relationship with God	Focuses on the detail – all the various sins we *think* we have committed
Leads to healthy remorse and then to praise and worship	Leads to unhealthy rumination and worry
Is felt more keenly with spiritual maturity, as we realize how human we are	Is felt most keenly when distant from God, and we believe it keeps us there
Your notes:	
Your notes:	

wrongdoing. Jesus has both paid the price *and* restored our relationship with God, something we will look at more in the next chapter, but, first, here are two ways in which true guilt can be *unhelpfully* managed.

Lack of guilt

Some people do not seem to feel guilt of any kind – true or false. They suppress it deep down, to where it is no longer felt at all. This might sound useful – but actually it robs you of the ability to have any true relationships. Effective relationships require the ability to feel remorse and learn from it – people who can't do this will leave a trail of brokenness behind them. By choosing to suppress your guilt, you are deciding to ignore your conscience. You are robbed of your inner moral compass – which subsequently distances you from most other people, who of course still have one.

The technical term for this inability to feel or learn from remorse is 'psychopathy', literally meaning 'the sick soul'.[3] The word 'psychopathic' has unhelpfully been linked to a stereotype of the mass murderer in recent years; in fact, psychopathic traits occur in many of us. These may make some people seem thick-skinned – most chief executives of large companies are often like this to some extent – but any major dose of psychopathy will lead to a very dysfunctional life. If this could be you, we would encourage you to talk to your GP or see an experienced counsellor. (See Appendix 2, p. 180 for more on how to do this.)

Disputable matters

There is a tendency for moral frameworks to change over time, as people relabel things as OK that were once thought of as wrong. This is not to say that the church should never change culturally – for example, there have been significant and helpful shifts in the roles of music and women. However, there are some things that the Bible says are morally wrong, which modern society can try to brush under the carpet.

At the same time, there are some common 'dilemmas' that face Christians today, including advances in bioengineering and what we choose to do on Sundays, which can be quite contentious. It is not the role of this book to take sides in these debates,[4] but, logically, these will result in some Christians feeling guilty when many in our society would not. However, we believe this is part of what it means to use discernment and to respond to the Bible in the light of personal conviction. We will cover this issue in more detail in chapter 3.

False guilt

True guilt is always against God, but false guilt can arise from a number of causes. For some readers, it might be helpful to see false guilt explained in more detail, so here is a simple breakdown. If this does not click with you, don't worry – you don't need to sub-categorize your false guilt to benefit from the rest of this book.

Some of you will have heard the old way of dividing up sins into those of 'commission' (things we have done, like stealing), sins of 'omission' (things we have not done, like not helping someone in need) and sins of 'poor stewardship' (things we have neglected, like not looking after the environment, or tolerating a rich/poor divide).[5] A similar threefold approach can be used to look at false guilt.

1. Guilt at something we think we have done wrong

Because guilt and uncertainty go hand in hand, if you struggle with guilt, you will probably have a list of things you *think* you have done that were wrong.

- These could be very minor things that no-one else would think are wrong, like going to the supermarket and getting everything on a long shopping list except that pack of butter. Yet, you berate yourself for your stupidity.
- You could also be jumping to conclusions and mind-reading. For example, someone you know walks past you in the street without saying 'hello'. You interpret this as proof that you must have offended them last time you spoke. You go over and over your last conversation[6] and (not surprisingly) come up with some things you could have said in a different way.

There are many more examples, but the common theme is assuming you have done something wrong because of your mood state or unhelpful thinking style, whereas in actual fact nothing happened, or certainly not anything that most people would feel guilty about. Once the downward spiral starts, it can be hard to stop it.

2. Guilt at something we have not done, but no harm has come about

You don't need to do something wrong to have a good go at yourself! Even the apostle Paul, reflecting upon the struggle he faces to meet the standards of the law, says, 'I do not do the good I want to do . . .' (Romans 7:19). Very often the standards we seek to reach differ from our eventual actions – standards are aspirational; actions are the results in day-to-day life.

However, our moral standards can be part of the problem, especially if they are stricter than God would have them be. These standards are typically formed from kernels of truth from biblical principles, but then overlaid with additional rules and clauses. Jesus accused the Jewish leaders of doing this at a meal in which they demonstrated their surprise when he did not engage in ritual washing: 'You experts in the law, woe to you, because you load people down with burdens they can hardly carry' (Luke 11:46). Today, we are equally good at putting these burdens on ourselves.

Spotting these unhelpfully high standards is tricky, because both the guilty person and the good Christian will want to have high standards. 'Be holy, because I am holy' (1 Peter 1:16) is often quoted, and this is a worthy call, but it can also become an excuse for beating ourselves up – something the original writers would not have wanted.[7]

As a pastor and a psychiatrist, we spend a lot of time listening to people describe their inner worlds. A few words stand out when we meet people who are like this. They are the imperatives: 'should', 'must', 'ought', 'always', 'never'. When such words are frequently present, it is time to stop and examine if this is really the case. Few things in life are so certain, and God's grace will not be limited by our grammar.

We can slip into habits in our thoughts – but stop for a moment. Have you noticed yourself saying any of these things?

- I **should** always be ready for anything that might happen
- I **must** be a good friend whenever anyone calls
- I **ought** to have seen that coming
- I **always** make sure nothing bad will happen
- I **never** allow chance to play a part

Logically, we know these things are unrealistic, like King Canute trying to stop the tide coming in,[8] but we continue to trot them out as reasons for doing more than we need – and as some small token to ease the guilt we feel.

This comes back to high standards – comparing ourselves to other people and perhaps 'going for a sainthood'. The reality of course is that, due to understandable fatigue or the sheer inability to be in two places at once, something may have happened that was less than ideal, but it was not for want of trying. Here are some special examples of this type of 'omission' guilt that deserve a mention:

- Survivor guilt: people who have survived hostage situations or wars when others have not, or people who have lost loved ones from suicide[9] might look back at things they could have done differently. Could the former have cried more loudly for help or have offered themselves instead? How can they ever live a happy life now when others have no life at all?
- Parental guilt: all parents are to some degree plagued by the feeling that they could be doing more for their children. Sometimes there is a specific focus, like whether they should go back to work or why other mums or dads have more money and buy more toys. Parental guilt is so common that we have devoted a section to it in chapter 4.
- Carer guilt: people who give of their time and energy to charities or to the care of relatives can find it hard to switch off – there is always so much more you could do. Church leaders are good examples of this, for the work is limitless, and burn-out often results.

3. Guilt that does not arise from specific acts, but is more diffuse, collective or free-floating

Some people just seem to feel guilty – they don't need to consider specific things they have done. The verdict appears to be 'guilty until proven innocent', and personal history provides a permanent backing-track to these feelings. Of course, as Christians we are fully aware of the fact that 'all have sinned and fall short of the glory of God' (Romans 3:23). Our pasts are littered with things that we have done wrong, things for which it was appropriate to feel truly guilty. Yet, having been forgiven and set free, sometimes decades ago, many Christians wrestle with a diffuse mist of badness.

Largely, the historical memories become a validation for the current feelings of guilt that have appeared. That's to say, 'I feel guilty; now what have I to feel guilty about? Ah yes, I remember now.' In this way, historic and resolved true guilt can be awakened by a feeling of guilt that may have absolutely no connection to these historic events. This sort of false guilt is very painful and exhausting, and we must first ask, not, 'What did I do?' but 'Why these feelings?'

No book on guilt would be complete without a brief mention of Sigmund Freud, who had a theory on this subject. He believed that growing up from child to adult involved a negotiation between our inner destructive desires and the moral society we have to join. At times on this journey, we internalize our destructive power – better to limit ourselves than harm those we want to be like. The pop psychologists call this 'teenage angst', and we normally grow out of it. If our development is arrested, for example, by a childhood trauma, the guilt can stay around, and all we can do is try to suppress it, which doesn't work very well[10] – the guilt still bubbles away underneath.

Mary was the favourite when she was young, and indeed her strict parents seemed to dislike her hyperactive brother. However, she was also seen as precious and vulnerable – likely to catch colds. She enjoyed receiving the attention, but knew she was no better than her brother. In fact, she felt she was probably worse – it was just that no-one had found her out yet. Mary ruminated on some of the bad thoughts that she had experienced and some of the selfish mistakes she had made. She felt guilty and like a fraud all of the time, but on the outside she looked happy and confident.

Derek was one of the few wealthy teenagers at a school in a relatively deprived area. Whenever there was any reference to poverty, Derek was showered with sarcastic remarks and put-downs. The cultural anger of his classmates had become his free-floating guilt. He was sure he must have done something terrible to feel this guilty, but he just couldn't work out what it was.

This kind of free-floating guilt can also come upon us later in life, often when our fundamental assumptions are challenged. For most of us, good mental health contains core beliefs like: 'I am a moral and decent person' or 'I am a competent nurse / teacher / cook . . .' These are based on fundamental assumptions, such as: 'the world is a safe place', 'the world has meaning' and 'people are worth something'. These are not universally held, but they are what most people living in the West believe deep down. Most Christians find their faith enhances them, as God's love and purposes are seen.

However, when catastrophe comes to the unsuspecting, these assumptions are shattered.[11] We say things like: 'this should not have happened' or 'I must have been incompetent'. Our assumptions are changed and our morality is brought into question, as we might not be as decent or capable as we had thought we were. If we think we are to blame, it becomes logical to assume that God does not love us any more.

Because our past attempt at understanding the world seems to have led us to this place, we can shy away again and again from trying to understand it. In the words of the 'Teacher' of Ecclesiastes, 'Everything is meaningless' (1:2), and, like the Teacher, we are somehow to blame. Guilt is the residue.

Type spotting

It can be hard to define which choices should lead to true guilt and which can result in false guilt. One reason for this is that many examples of mistakes that cause true guilt become quickly overlaid with false guilt as we compound the original problem. Conversely, as you deal with some false guilt, you may realize that it was acting as a distraction from some true guilt you needed to take to Jesus for forgiveness.

Essential in this process is the transformation of our *human conscience*. In the Bible, we read of how we must hold on to 'faith and a good conscience' (1 Timothy 1:19). As we come to know biblical teachings and the nature of God better, so we become more able to discern right and wrong – and to develop a *Christian conscience* that is rooted in the objective truth of Scripture.

Please pause and do the following exercise. In the list opposite, please say whether each action is one that should lead to true or false guilt. Write your responses in the *right-hand* column.

How easy did you find it to complete? Which items were you wanting to say, 'Yes, but . . .' to?

⇨*Notes:*

_____
_____
_____

Example	True or false?
Stealing money from someone	
Stealing from the rich to give to the poor	
Hitting someone in the face when they have done nothing wrong	
Hitting someone in the face when they are about to attack you	
Feeling guilty on behalf of your son who has been in a fight	
Feeling guilty when you see a film about slavery	
Not voting in an election because you feel your vote will not count	
Not voting in an election because you cannot leave your house	
Not having stood up for your mother when your father came home drunk	
Not having intervened while someone was attacked by a gang near you	
Enjoying the act of doing something wrong	
Enjoying wishing ill-will to someone who was unkind to you	
Living your life as if God did not exist	
Living your life as if you were responsible for everything around you	
Living your life as quietly as possible, so as not to get in people's way	

Taking action: noticing guilty thoughts

The first step in tackling false guilt is to notice when such thoughts are present. You will have some that keep on coming into your head – most of us have 'guilt themes' that are well-worn paths of self-accusation.

In the table opposite, write down some guilty thoughts that often come into your head. You might want to keep a simple diary for a few days to generate these. Keep the diary short, perhaps as a deletable digital file. Then try to stand back and decide if these thoughts are examples of true or false guilt. If you think the thought is a mix of both true and false guilt, divide it into two thoughts, as in the example below:

> A combined true-and-false thought that is too broad and non-specific to be clear:
> 'I have let my friends down.'
>
> Separated into two separate and more specific thoughts:
> True guilt: 'I have let Richard down by not replying to his important email.'
> False guilt: 'I tend to let my friends down a lot.'

Having a thought does not mean you believe it with full certainty. If 100% means that you believe it completely, 25% would mean that you believe it only a little, like a nagging suspicion. You can use a different scale if you wish.[12]

In the final column, try to write down how you feel as a result of a specific guilty thought. We have suggested a scale from 1 to 10, where 1 is feeling very bad and 10 is feeling fine, and again, use a different scale if you wish.

Guilty thought	True or false?	Strength of belief 0–100%	Mood 1–10

The idea here is to realize that we rarely believe all our thoughts 100%. Instead, there is a range of belief – and hence a range of emotional responses we can make use of. It is not all 100% awful!

It can be quite scary actually to write things down like this, almost as though putting them in black and white makes them true or confirms that you are a bad person after all. However, please remember that this is just an exercise, and the first step in the trip out of guilt. Also, when you do write things down, you might be able to say that you don't believe them that much after all.

Summary

In this chapter, we have seen that guilt is complex but that it can helpfully be divided into two types: false and true. We have looked at true guilt, and the importance of a moral framework to guide this. We then looked in more detail at false guilt and began to note our guilty thoughts and the extent to which we believed them.

Exercises

In the spaces below, record your answers to help you understand your starting point in your trip out of guilt.

What one thing did you read in this chapter that was new and
helpful?

_____

_____

_____

What one thing did you struggle to understand?

_____

_____

_____

About your table of guilty thoughts:
- What was your most strongly believed guilty thought?

  _____

  _____

- What was a thought that you believed a bit but not that
  much?

  _____

  _____

- How do these thoughts differ?

  _____

  _____

Complete this sentence: If guilt were less of a problem for
me, I would . . .

1. _____

2. _____

3. _____

2. Guilty as sin – and how true guilt is healed

Never let us be guilty of sacrificing any portion of truth
on the altar of peace.
J. C. Ryle[1]

This chapter may be the most important collection of words you have ever read. Or it may serve merely to compound your frustration that the so-called 'good news' of the Christian gospel cannot shift your guilty feelings. To put it another way, this chapter will enable you to determine whether your problems are with true guilt or false guilt. We will also ask why we so often seek to hide our guilt from God, and consider the value of confession in recovery. If it is true guilt that you are wrestling with, this chapter will outline the only means by which you can break free, and offer you the tools to put that recovery into practice.

The second half of this chapter seeks to unpack areas in which the church has confused the message of recovery from true guilt or where it has propagated a new guilt entirely. This section is particularly important to consider if you have found your experience of guilt to be deeply entwined with your experience of the church.

Fig leaf, anyone?

Right from the start of the Christian story, we have tried to hide ourselves, or specific things, from God. In the book of Genesis, chapter 3, we see how Adam and Eve hide their nakedness from God (verse 7) and then themselves (verse 8). Hiding from God is completely ineffective, but we try it anyway because sometimes it is too painful to face him.

The idea that God will somehow burn us up if we are fully honest with him is one that has crept into our religion. It seems logical, for God is so holy. In the Old Testament, there is the story of Moses having to hide in a cleft in a rock while God passed by (Exodus 33:19–23). But if you read this story carefully, it is clear that God is actually being very gracious, allowing Moses to experience only what he knows he can bear.

Throughout the Bible, God welcomes those who confess their wrongs to him and he forgives them. If anything, God is more likely to be angry with us when we are dishonest with him.[2] But none of this stops us from hiding our guilt and trying to shift the blame. Adam blames Eve, Eve blames the serpent – and the serpent doesn't have a leg to stand on . . .

The great twist in Genesis 3 is not only that God can see straight through any fig leaf, but that he actually makes a better covering for Adam and Eve in the form of some animal skins (verse 21). To obtain animal skins, you have to kill an animal, and this is the first example in the Bible of a blood sacrifice – where the blood of one thing covers over the guilt of another. This begins a theme that runs throughout the Bible, culminating in Jesus' blood being spilt to pay for our sins.

In order to benefit from the clothing God can supply, we have to commit to come out of hiding and remove our own attempts to cover ourselves. Ephesians 4:22–23 says, 'Put off your old self . . . put on the new self . . .' Despite the offer of being reclothed by God, very often we have become overly attached to our old 'fig leaves'. These destructive ways of coping then become a blockage to our opportunity to find true freedom.

Suppression of guilty feelings is the most common way through which we try to hide our guilt from God. A classical example of this in the Bible is where King David has been suspending his morals. Over a whole chapter (2 Samuel 11), he lusts after Bathsheba, sleeps with her, tries to trick her husband and then arranges to have him killed. It is not until Nathan the prophet confronts him (chapter 12) that he wakes up to reality. In a psalm, he confesses his sin again not only against them, but also against God:

> Finally, I confessed all my sins to you
>   and stopped trying to hide my guilt.
> I said to myself, 'I will confess my rebellion to the LORD.'
> (Psalm 32:5 NLT)

Most readers of this book will not have tried to have someone killed, but being open about our tendency to suppress and hide our guilt is an important first step in dealing with it. As we saw earlier, the Bible is clear that all have sinned and, in doing so, fallen short of God's standard (Romans 3:23) – we are 'as guilty as sin' – and the degree or manner of our falling is not discussed.

True guilt: a healing framework

Throughout history and across every religious framework there has existed a hope of redemptive healing from guilt.

Every culture has seen the emotion of guilt as a sign that something is wrong and has sought to make amends for it in some way. As such, guilt is a good thing – if it leads us towards a better way. Galatians 3:24 says that, in the Old Testament, 'The law was put in charge of us until Christ came that we might be justified by faith' – meaning that one role of these rules and regulations was to point out the need for a better and higher way called Jesus.

> Several years ago, while skiing in Switzerland, I got terribly lost within a blanket snowstorm. After some time, I found myself within a huge forest, unable to ski down and equally unable to climb back out. I knew that steep cliffs lay in most directions. When the gravity of my situation began to register, I was gripped by such a deep terror that I began to cry. I was filled with remorse for not taking greater care and deep regret at not making better provision for avalanche or self-preservation. Regaining my composure, I started to try to navigate an escape – not easy in a pine forest, in a snowstorm and in failing light.
>
> I prayed for God's help and within minutes had identified two short fence posts slightly closer together than the others nearby. Barbed wire connected all of these other posts in the banked snow, but when I swept my hand through the snow between these two closer posts, there was no wire. Hope sparked within me as I sensed that this gap could only demark a path. Reckoning a rough line forward, and at times wading through waist-deep snow, I arrived three hours later with great relief at a train line and was able to return safely to my hotel.

True guilt is a universal human experience. We all find ourselves caught in the storms of life and sooner or later tearfully lost in a forest of guilt, regret and remorse. We are presented with hundreds of paths to escape these feelings, but none of them can heal us, and some of them even lead directly to death.

What then are the characteristics of the 'better way', of something that can lead us out of danger to live well, love deeply and forgive much? Below are three essentials to a genuine healing framework for true guilt:

1. Acknowledgment

Denial, repression or suppression of our true guilt will never change our experience of guilt. We need to learn not to hide from our guilt, yet the reality is that many people struggle to fully acknowledge that they are guilty at all. In theory, they know it to be true (perhaps because they have read the Bible), but how do we accept this in our hearts?

What we are seeking in this acknowledgment is a plain and honest recognition before God of those things that we have thought, said or done that have hurt our neighbour, damaged ourselves or been wrong in the eyes of God.

You may find it painful to bring to mind the mistakes of your past. However, this unmasking work is essential if the real pain of true guilt is to be dealt with. Time is no healer for true guilt, and so putting off acknowledgment merely delays the inevitable. Try asking God in prayer for a revelation of your true sin. This is a safe and real way of separating those things that are significant from those things that are insignificant.

2. Atonement

This is a technical term, meaning 'at-one-ment' – that is, the ability for us to be one in relationship with God again (at one with him) and no longer separated by sin. Another term for this is 'absolution', deriving from the Latin *absolutionem*, meaning 'completion, acquittal'.

Forgiveness appeals to the emotions, but atonement is a more forensic term, and the Christian healing framework offers something far greater than simple relief from guilty feelings. It offers a material change in our spiritual status, removing our guilt in its totality, with all of its debts, dues and penalties.

Hebrews 10:22 says, 'Let us draw near to God with a sincere heart in full assurance of faith, having our hearts sprinkled to cleanse us from a guilty conscience and having our bodies washed with pure water.' There are a number of other metaphors for atonement used in the Bible, such as moving from being orphans to being adopted into God's family.[3]

3. Authority

Any effective healing model for the truly guilty is dependent upon the ultimate authority behind it. The ultimate authority here is God – because he is the One sinned against and he is the One who upholds the moral fabric of the universe. This is why humans cannot forgive in the same way as God can. This is illustrated in the following example:

> If I take a large hammer to the car that always steals the parking space outside our house and I then ask a *friend* to forgive me for the damage I have caused to the car (whose owner I do not know), can that friend forgive me? He can certainly make me feel better (as my confession to him will make my conscience feel a bit lighter), but in material terms I remain guilty – in the eyes of the

law, the car-owner and the owner's insurance company. Not to mention spiritually . . .

If, however, I stand by the car and acknowledge my guilt for this act of destruction to the *owner* of the vehicle, the person with direct authority, whose property I have damaged, has the opportunity to forgive me. There may also be a cost to pay and possibly a court to face, all of which reflect the consequences of the real act I am responsible for and the authorities I am legally answerable to. And as well as confessing to a person, I should also seek forgiveness from God.

Please note that, even if I secured forgiveness from the owner of the car and paid my fine to the courts, my guilt would not necessarily be satisfied, nor would I feel fully forgiven. If you have spent any time in prisons or working with ex-offenders, you will know that despite 'doing time', and in some cases being directly forgiven by the victims of their crimes, true guilt can remain. There has to be an authority far beyond those we have wronged and even beyond the judicial system for our guilt to be truly atoned (or paid) for. This is because wrongdoing, or 'sin' if we use the traditional Christian term, is multidirectional and has wider consequences. It is not merely a transaction between aggressor and victim.

When we sin, we express our inhumanity. It breaks our own hearts as much as it breaks the hearts of others. It seems to cause a rift in the very fabric of our world. Ultimately, the only authority that can forgive me for the damage I have caused to humanity (mine and others) is the author of humanity itself: God. The Christian healing model is complete because only God can heal completely.

Psalm 103:12 says,

> As far as the east is from the west,
>   so far has he removed our transgressions from us.

The finality of the forgiveness that God offers me separates me from my sin, not by means of time, memory or by distraction, but in a cosmological manner available only to the Lord of the universe. I need this forgiveness not because I can understand it, but precisely because it is too grand for me to understand.

Exercise

Bring to mind a minor way in which you have wronged someone else. Write down a list of everyone who was affected and underline everyone who held any authority to offer you forgiveness.

⇨ My list:

_____

_____

_____

_____

True guilt – true punishment

It is very unfashionable to talk about punishment today, both within the context of psychology and within many Christian traditions. Instead, we tend to focus upon the ideas of recovery or restoration from guilt. This is despite the fact that there is something intrinsic to the human spirit that craves punishment for the things we have done wrong.

If you find yourself rereading the preceding sentence, I am sure you are not alone. We tend to assume that everyone wants to run away from punishment and hide their guilt. This is, on the surface, true. However, could it be that whilst punishment may sometimes be feared, it can also be a welcome resolution? In my role as a minister, I (Will) have heard countless confessions of penitent men and women who have finally staggered through my door to confess their guilty secrets, containing words to the effect of: 'I just cannot carry this burden any more. I need to confess and face the consequences.'

Every person, Christian or not, shares these sorts of feelings. In 1995, Clive White claimed the record for the largest trout caught in the UK, yet eight years later he wrote the following email to the British Fishing Records Committee:

> From: Clive White
> Sent: 16 July 2003 12:26
> Subject: Withdraw Claim
> July 16, 2003
>
> Dear Mr Rowe
>
> I would like to take this opportunity to withdraw my claim to the BFRC in connection with the Record Rainbow Trout caught.
> The Record in question was the current British Record Rainbow Trout caught at Dever Springs Trout Fishery on 4 April 1995, weighing 36lb 14oz 8drm (16.740kg). I did not catch the fish; it was all set up so there would be a new British Record. The fish was not even stocked into the lake; it was actually placed in a bag next to the lake all ready for me to claim.

> I am very sorry and deeply regret what I have done, but I cannot live a lie any more, as it has destroyed my marriage and it very nearly destroyed me. As a result, I have now given up fishing all together. I know a lot of people will take a dim view of what I have done, but now I can sleep at night, knowing that I have nothing to hide. I feel sorry for the people that I have cheated out of a genuine Record Claim. I only hope people will respect me for coming clean and telling the truth.
>
> Yours sincerely
>
> Clive White

In the vast majority of confessions I have heard, there has been no need to take any action beyond hearing the confession and explaining the Christian response, but even then, some individuals suggest that they would feel better if they could be punished for their mistake. This, unfortunately, can be the beginning of false guilt, where the desire for punishment morphs into the use of guilt as a punishment (more on this later).

The Christian healing framework for guilt does not divorce punishment from recovery. In fact, the Christian healing framework places a high value on punishment because it identifies the priority of justice in God himself. In Christian terms, there is no atonement without punishment, and, by that token, God determined both to rule for punishment and receive the penalty himself. John 3:16 says, 'For God so loved the world, that he gave his one and only Son, that whoever believes in him shall not perish but have eternal life.'

Jesus Christ, God's perfect Son, died on the cross to pay the price for your sin and mine. He bore the punishment that every single truly guilty person in the world would ever deserve. As it says in Isaiah 53:5,

> He was pierced for our transgressions,
> > he was crushed for our iniquities;
> the punishment that brought us peace was on him,
> > and by his wounds we are healed.

This may offend our Western sensibilities,[4] but in our journey away from guilt, we need to know just how fully and completely God has dealt with our wrongdoing.

Exercise

Write down your responses to the following:
- How you felt when you became fully aware of your true guilt

_____

_____

_____

- How you felt able to distinguish between things for which you believed you needed God's forgiveness versus those things you felt were not significant

_____

_____

_____

Getting personal

The true guilt that many people carry is a far greater weight than the embarrassment or humiliation they fear in

acknowledging their guilt. This can leave people suffering
needlessly for years with a toxic burden to carry. As Clive
White showed in his email, carrying hidden guilt isn't freeing:
it actually cost him his marriage and nearly his sanity.
Ultimately, true guilt is truly personal and it's personal to God.

Two of the underpinning values of Western culture are
independence and self-sufficiency. The difficulty with this
culture is that it clashes directly with the Christian healing
model for guilt that is dependent upon a personal acknowledgment of our wrongdoings (sins) and a decision to accept
God's help in being restored. Some try to work their own way
out of true guilt. We would argue that their attempts are
ultimately flawed from the beginning since they lack the
authority for *atonement*.

Receiving the benefit of the Christian healing model for
guilt is dependent upon a person's humility in recognizing
their shortcomings and accepting God's gracious forgiveness.
It is not a complex process, but it is a complete and an absolute
one. Regardless of any of the possible human consequences
to our errors, God's atonement rehumanizes us, restores us,
pays the debt for us and provides us with peace. Ultimately
and most importantly, it is not a transaction in a vacuum, but
a relationship that occurs with profound love: the love that
God has for each one of us as his precious children.

The personal prayer

A prayer for someone who would like to benefit from the
Christian healing model for true guilt would look something
like the one opposite.[5] Can you 'get personal' and pray this
prayer? Rather than just reading it, we encourage you to write
it out on a card and put it where you will see it often. This
could be on the bathroom mirror or even on the back of the
toilet door.

Dear Father God,

I recognize my true guilt: the things that I have done, thought and said that have offended you, hurt my neighbour and damaged myself. I have tried to run and hide from the reality of these things, but I cannot carry the burden any longer. Today, I acknowledge my sin. I recognize your authority over me and I accept that the punishment that I deserve was laid upon your Son Jesus Christ, for my sake. I receive the forgiveness that you offer me now and I invite your Holy Spirit to dwell in my heart. Remove my guilt as you have promised and fill me with grace and thankfulness.

In Jesus' name,
Amen.

Religious confusion

We have sought to make the Christian healing model for true guilt as plain as is possible in the previous paragraphs. The need for this clarity is a large part of our motivation for writing this book. Christians remain plagued by guilt's presence and confused about how to reconcile their enduring feelings with God's atoning work. More than that, at times the church has compounded the problem of true guilt with emphases that fuel the conditions within which false guilt can thrive.

The remainder of this book is concerned with clearing away the smoke and mirrors of false or lingering guilt, in order that we might share in the raw delight that the Christian healing model provides. I am heartened by Martin Luther who initiated the Reformation in 1517, primarily in response to the then distorted approach to atonement.[6] Having spent years in bondage to false guilt and reflecting upon the simple message of atonement in the book of Galatians, he says, 'This . . . gives singular comfort to the consciences of all who are terrified at the greatness of their sins. However invincible a tyrant sin is, Christ has overcome it through his death, and it cannot hurt those who believe in him.'[7]

How sad that so many Christians have struggled to feel this comfort, and that so many of those who don't attend church perceive it as a place that will *cause* them to have a guilt problem, not a place that will *release* them from one! We will return to Luther in future chapters, but for now let's identify three of the key confusions that the church has lent to the resolution of a guilty conscience.

1. Our general guilt culture

Anthropology suggests that 'guilt cultures' are created as a means of social control.[8] Within these cultures, people are controlled by their taking part in the behaviours of that group. For example, they gossip as the (seemingly) only way to combat all the gossip that goes on around them. Their desire to remain included in the group means that they do things they would not otherwise do (causing guilt), and they are haunted by the potential to be rejected (causing shame). In most guilt cultures, people feel 'bad' most of the time, but they aren't sure why, and these cultures force people into secrecy, as they fear the scrutiny of their peers.

There is no doubt that Christianity has been used as a weapon of cultural control at various times over the last 2,000 years. You need only a cursory understanding of Roman history to know that this is true.[9] Sadly, on a smaller level, individual churches can propagate control through guilt. In its worst guises, this is justified as 'discipleship'. However, it is not hard to distinguish between 'biblical discipleship' and what is actually 'guilt-based cultural control'. You may well have heard the term 'heavy shepherding' to describe this type of destructive ministry.

Biblical discipleship	Guilt-based control
Motivated by a desire to please God and fuelled by joy	Motivated by the fear of exclusion and rejection
Propagates honesty and openness	Propagates secrecy and false/true self divisions
Confession is a joy	Confession is terrifying
Does not fear humiliation or exclusion	Humiliation and gossip are common
Anticipates restoration and forgiveness	Anticipates heavy discipline/punishment
Leads to forgiveness and a light conscience	Leads to engrained false guilt and apprehension
Sees people move on in faith and grow in ministry	Sees people remain static in faith, and responsibility remains centrally held

2. Atonement through works

Ephesians 2:8–9 says, 'For it is by grace you have been saved, through faith – and this is not from yourselves, it is the gift of God – not by works, so that no-one can boast.' Despite the clarity of this verse, different parts of the church have upheld the importance of 'good works' in the atonement process. The biblical narrative is not all one-sided, as you will see from James 2:24: 'You see that people are justified by what they do and not by faith alone', but to emphasize works over faith is to miss the central point of the gospel message.

Consider your own religious background. Were you made to feel as if you had to earn your way to heaven? All parts of the Christian church have made mistakes in this area. As well as being theologically dubious, linking works to atonement has catastrophic consequences for the guilt problem. It propagates a culture in which most of the congregation feel that they 'aren't doing enough' and never will.

There have been breaks away from this belief (such as the Reformation described above, and a subsequent Counter-Reformation[10]). Some denominations have changed hugely (for the better), but echoes of an emphasis on justification through works can still remain within them.

It is because of this feeling that false guilt has sometimes been labelled 'Catholic Guilt'. You may have heard the saying: 'No-one does guilt like a Catholic' – many Catholics will smile at this (and still flinch inside!). There is something about the way that some churches handle confession that keeps guilt going, rather than setting it free.

This theological distortion also arises within Protestant churches, even though the very denomination was created as a 'protest' to this issue. Consider:

- The quiet rural Anglican parish church where a strict hierarchy prevails, and no-one lets 'Joan' forget that she once arrived quite late for church.
- Or did you see the Charismatic worship centre where everyone appeared to express 'supernatural gifts'? Well, not everyone, there were quite a few who didn't seem quite ready for those blessings.

- Then there was the zealous city Bible-teaching church where only some seemed to have the knack of studying Scripture with enjoyment. Only they were given leadership roles and the opportunity to take on small groups.

We are assuming that if you go to a church where you feel like this, we won't need to spell out the specifics. Our aim here is to show you that the problem is sadly widespread (just as it is down at the golf club or at the local pub) and that it was never God's wish for how his people should relate.

> Every year I (Will) run a course called Alpha that invites people to explore the Christian faith for themselves. Within the first session of the course, I always invite the delegates to speak publicly about their most negative assumptions and misgivings about the Christian church.
>
> Without fail, several people will say things along the lines of: 'The church will make you feel guilty. I feel bad enough as it is!' I then make a public apology on behalf of the church to everyone for whom that is in any way true.

Surely a God of love is seeking a response of love to his act of love? Therefore, it is hard to believe that his intention would be to 'guilt' people into acts of service. Indeed, to participate in acts of service on the basis of fear or reward would seem at odds with the whole essence of Jesus' teaching. John 15:12 says, 'My command is this: love each other as I have loved you.'

3. Churches and legalism

Much of Jesus' ministry was spent criticizing the legalistic and compassionless approach of the religious leaders of the day. Paul follows this approach by challenging those who tried to move the church back towards the Old Testament law. He says in Galatians 5:4, 'You who are trying to be justified by the law have been alienated from Christ; you have fallen away from grace.'

If Paul's letters give us any clues as to a battle for the heart of the church, it was always going to be fought over the balance between liberty and legalism. Too much liberty, and worship becomes disorderly and sin creeps in; too much legalism, and grace is lost and guilt pervades.

The balance between these two polarities is not just reflected within the church, but also within the human spirit. We will talk in the next chapter about the 'Guilt and Shame Proneness Scale', which reveals that some people are hard-wired towards self-imposed legalism, while others have dominant liberality. Churches can find themselves (usually because of the wiring of their leader, and consequently those whom they attract) leaning strongly in either direction. Of course, all will say that they are simply responding to God in obedience, but this is very rarely the case. The Lord calls us to holiness but not to legalism, and to freedom but not liberalism.

Legalism creates a strong sense of general inadequacy in churches, and it is this underlying resignation to 'being a failure' that makes guilt so pervasive. We are all sinners, to be sure (that is the main requirement for becoming a Christian!), but the Christian healing model never intended that people would remain bound to guilt and self-loathing.

Legalistic church cultures are different from 'guilt-based control cultures', because the intention of the leadership is rarely to manipulate or control. Very often, the leaders are genuinely struggling with a sense of personal unworthiness, which in turn leads them to distort biblical teaching on righteousness at the expense of grace. But being 'prone' to legalism does not give them a mandate to hurt people when they express it.

Christian legalism can make you feel guilty in the most trivial of situations, such as sitting in the wrong seat or letting your baby cry during Communion. It's hard to get this right, since most churches have some dos and don'ts that are very peculiar. But, because you are in a church, you immediately apply a moral filter to this and think you have offended God. People find themselves feeling terrible for things that actually have no moral value at all. They start asking nervously, 'Have I done something wrong? I feel that I am not good enough to worship here.'

We hope, pray and trust that most churches are actually OK, but we are truly sorry if you have suffered with guilt as a result of these distortions. Is there any way in which we can apologize on their behalf and encourage you to try again?

A word about atheists and guilt

One seemingly obvious way to get rid of guilt is to get rid of God. After all, it could be argued that much of the guilt that Christians suffer from arises from worries about how/if/when we have offended God. However, this is not as simple as it seems.

Firstly, this idea is based on the concept that it is a good thing to get rid of an external morality. This is not as brilliant an idea as it might seem, as everything suddenly becomes relative. Now the atrocities of Adolf Hitler or Genghis Khan have as much validity as stories of freedom and hope. Atheists

typically respond that they do have a morality which arises
from the 'community' (a bit like democracy).[11] The difficulty
with this is that many things can arise from a community.
(Remember William Golding's book *Lord of the Flies?*[12]) If
all truth is relative, then this is no more than stepping out on
your own. Adolf and Genghis become no more than people
walking out of step with the herd.

Secondly, as will be our main argument in this book, the
worries of most Christians are based on false and not true
guilt. The answer to religious guilt is not to remove religion,
but to see how much God really loves us and forgives
our true guilt, and then to put false guilt back where it
belongs – in the bin! Our beliefs need to be redeemed, not
abandoned.

Summary

Earlier in this chapter we highlighted Psalm 103:12 which
says,

> As far as the east is from the west,
>   so far has he removed our transgressions [guilt] from us.

This is a remarkable promise – and one that is offered only
through the Christian healing model explained in the first half
of this chapter. This is such a supreme offer; we would suggest
that no amount of diversion and distraction should weaken
your resolve to grasp it fully.

The Christian healing model is the only path to healing
from true guilt. As Jesus said of himself, 'I am the way [path]
and the truth and the life' (John 14:6). If you want to enjoy
recovery from guilt (and there is no other treatment available),
both Rob and I recommend this absolutely!

Exercises

Approximately what percentage of your overall guilty feelings do you believe are related to true guilt, as opposed to things that you feel inappropriately guilty for (false guilt)?

True guilt _____ % versus false guilt _____ %

Aside from the Christian healing model, can you think of any healthy means by which your guilt could be fully and finally dealt with?

_____

_____

_____

What struck you most about the AAA standard of the Christian healing model?

- Acknowledgment:

  _____

- Atonement:

  _____

- Authority:

  _____

What do you find hardest to accept about the way Jesus Christ resolves your true guilt through his sacrifice?

_____

_____

Have you, or might you, make the Christian healing model personal through the prayer on page 53?

_____

_____

3. Guilty by design – why false guilt flourishes

Unexpressed emotions will never die.
They are buried alive and
will come forth later in uglier ways.
Attributed to Sigmund Freud

I was once told a story about a family friend who borrowed her husband's original VW Beetle to make a long motorway trip. She had used the car several times before without a problem, but on this particular occasion she broke down by the side of the road. Going around to the front of the car, she opened the bonnet to see what might have happened. To her astonishment, there was no engine present. Calling the RAC, she explained that the engine must have fallen out of her husband's car and she had subsequently broken down. The RAC controller asked her what model of car she was driving, before politely explaining that the engine was in fact in the boot of the car.

Responding to false guilt is not unlike this story. Most people become aware that some of their guilt is disproportionate or completely false somewhere along their life journey. They splutter along, losing power or possibly even stopping altogether. Their guilty feelings lead them to believe that something catastrophic has happened (like the engine falling out). However, a little professional knowledge reveals that the problem is not what it appears to be and that it can be repaired.

In this chapter, we are going to help you take a look at the engine of your mind and see what keeps cycles of false guilt alive. We are then going to illustrate three different approaches to making engine repairs. Explaining these three different approaches may seem unnecessary, but we believe this level of understanding will give you confidence to use the tools we outline later in the book. These will work to prevent future 'false-guilt' breakdowns and leave you with greater peace of mind for the journey ahead.

The origins of guilt

Research among Western children has shown that feelings of guilt are first encountered between the ages of three and five years,[1] often when a child is learning greater independence and is unsure if something is allowed. This overlaps with the less developed emotion of shame, which occurs from around fifteen months and is more to do with wanting to keep things hidden.[2]

When the child experiences guilt, two things can happen: either the parent will tell him or her off or encourage the child to try again. A positive parenting response will focus on whatever the child is doing that is correct/safe/helpful. The parent will thus teach the child over time what is right and wrong,[3] and encourage the child to try new things or use more initiative. A negative parenting response will constantly criticize the child for doing things less than perfectly, and as a result the child not only fails to develop a sense of right and wrong (for everything is wrong), he or she also feels alone, guilty and ashamed. Instead of taking the initiative, the child becomes passive.

Alternatively, they may flee their guilt by pursuing a future goal (university, job, marriage, wealth, etc.) in an attempt to find approval. Ironically, this also fuels false guilt, as they sense a huge disparity between their outer success and inner sense of 'badness'. This sort of striving turns us from human beings into 'human doings'.

Three mechanisms for change

1. Psychoanalysis and the Analytical School

In 1900, Sigmund Freud[4] revolutionized how we thought about the brain by introducing the idea of the unconscious mind. Freud said that in the unconscious lay our most powerful and primitive emotions. Defence mechanisms, he said, could be called into play to hide some of the deep emotions, some healthy, like using art to access your inner passions, but some unhealthy, like denial or blaming things on other people.

Supportive and loving early relationships typically result in more healthy defence mechanisms. When this stability has not been present, there is more of a rift between the unconscious emotions and the conscious self. Less helpful defence mechanisms are then used like blunt instruments, and guilt is a common emotion here because we believe we are either evil or totally deficient.

In the treatment process of analytical psychotherapy, the therapist models a stable relationship to allow 'neurotic' guilt (their name for false guilt) to be processed and healthier defence mechanisms to be developed.

2. Cognitive therapy

Aaron Beck was an analytical psychotherapist by training, but over time he came to see that *what* and *how* people thought could actually be more important that any unconscious emotion they might be trying to cover up. In the 1960s, Beck developed a therapeutic model called Cognitive Behavioural Therapy (CBT), which has the added advantage of being easier to understand than Freud's theories, though both have their merits.

> Imagine you are a teacher in charge of a school group on a trip to a busy town centre. You hear an ambulance, and thoughts rush through your head: 'It is one of the children. I have not kept track of them. I have done something wrong, and now someone is hurt . . .' You can see how guilty emotions and self-reproach would follow – even in the time it takes you to run to the source of the siren.
>
> However, consider how your thinking would change if you knew that in the next street the local ambulance service were having an open day and had invited children to climb up into the vehicles. From time to time, they turn the siren on so visitors can hear just how loud it is.
>
> Do you feel as guilty now?

Cognitive therapists help us look at how our thoughts can so easily run away with themselves and lead us into guilty and depressed emotions. We will use a largely 'CBT-based' approach in the rest of this book.

3. Behavioural therapy

Some drivers for behaviour are sub-conscious and non-verbal. B. F. Skinner, the first behaviourist,[5] showed this with rats in the research lab. The idea was that if you have enough rewards

Type of guilt	Example of helpful approach
True	The Christian healing model has to be the core part of the approach here, as wrong has been done, and a price for sin must be paid. Yet, even true guilt can be overlaid with false guilt. This means that even if a person has been fully forgiven, they may struggle to feel it. This is where an integrated approach is helpful, with psychology playing a supportive role to the spiritual reality of the forgiveness we have found in Jesus Christ.
False	Cognitive Behavioural Therapy will help with seeing accurately what is going on. It is not about positive thinking or overlooking sin, but it is about challenging inaccurate thinking to see the true picture. After all, some people have a tendency to feel guilty all the time! It also contains techniques for managing tendencies to assume too much responsibility. There are also ways of managing this type of false guilt when you just can't be sure, because not all situations lend themselves to experiments. Behavioural therapy can help people change their behaviour in a simple and straightforward way. This can be very good for individuals who find it too painful to think deeply or who are too depressed to think clearly. It can also help with reinforcing new and better behaviours – and, as a result, new emotions. Psychotherapy can be helpful in seeing 'how' a false guilt arose. The healing relationship of psychotherapy can assist with experiencing trust for the first time – especially useful if there has been significant past trauma. Even if a person logically understands the gospel and how to tackle false guilt using CBT, it can be psychotherapy that will help them feel the forgiveness that is spiritually theirs.

in the form of food, or punishments in the form of electric shocks, the rat would do what you wanted it to do. But, as far as we know, rats do not think that deeply about what they are doing!

Guilt can be a great motivator, especially in the short term – just like an electric shock. We can sometimes achieve incredibly good things because of a twinge of guilt. However, as we know, guilt is not always a helpful or supportive emotion. Behavioural therapy in this sense is morally neutral.

Behavioural therapists can, however, help us to see where guilt can drive us towards negative things (like going back into destructive relationships), and then disempower this drive. They can help us set new targets and stimulate more healthy habits, pointing out the rewards along the way.

Circuits in the brain

Guilt results in physical changes to the brain. It is not an ethereal emotion, but something that can actually be seen on brain scans. A technique called 'functional magnetic resonance imaging' (or fMRI) uses chemicals to show which bits of the brain are most active at any time. Certain regions 'light up' when we are thinking guilty thoughts:[6] the interesting thing here is that these regions are the bit of the brain that also helps us stand back and get things in perspective. If we can't stand back, we will not be able to see the effect of our actions on others.

Disorders that reduce function in this part of the brain can mean that the healthy role of guilt is lost, and individuals can do things that seem harsh or cruel. Likewise, disorders that make this area overactive can result in unhealthy guilt: for example, in the case of obsessive compulsive disorder (see Appendix 2, p. 188), guilt can be overdeveloped, and people can find it hard to see they are not responsible for things far outside of their control. All these changes are visible in the brain and mean that the person cannot just 'snap out of it' – instead, some brain *retraining* will be needed.

The part of the brain that holds feelings of guilt and other emotions is called the 'limbic system'. This system 'sets the mind's emotional tone, filters external triggers, tags events as internally important and stores highly charged emotional memories'.[7] Unlike other parts of the brain that acquire facts quickly (like the list of things you have done today), the limbic system responds slowly. It needs healing relationships, the passage of time and new experiences, so explaining to someone *why* they should not feel guilty is not enough. We need to help people *feel* less guilty at a deeper and more profound level. And this will take time.

Guilt and clinical depression

The word 'depression' covers a very broad range of emotions and has lots of meanings. But as a psychiatrist, I (Rob) am very aware that there is a severe illness called 'clinical depression'[8] that, in its most extreme forms, can result in huge feelings of guilt. Here, the pathways and circuits described above have become so dominant that it is very hard to think a balanced thought or challenge false guilt.

If you are severely depressed, you should speak to your general practitioner (GP, or family doctor). They will be able to help with medication that can adjust the brain pathways and with access to skilled therapists to help you with the techniques in this book that you may struggle to use on your own. (See Appendix 2 for more information.)

> Doctors differentiate between a neurotic type of depression, where you are still able to think with some perspective, albeit with difficulty, and 'psychotic' depression, where you have lost touch with reality and believe that things are 100% bad. Psychotic depression can be very scary, as people can believe very dark things, such as that all the world's guilt is literally stored up in them. If this describes you or someone you know, do please seek *urgent* help.

Guilt proneness

In 2011, a helpful psychological study was released by Taya R. Cohen of the Carnegie Mellon University in Pittsburgh called 'The Guilt and Shame Proneness Scale' (GASP for short).[9] The focus was to assist in indicating which sorts of people would engage in less ethical behaviour, but conversely identified that 30%–40% of the population have 'high guilt proneness' (regardless of their religious convictions). These individuals are far more likely to suffer from an oversensitive conscience than their low-scoring counterparts who, at the most extreme end, struggle to experience any guilt at all.

Genetics cannot provide a complete answer as to why some people struggle with false guilt and others do not. However, it is very helpful to recognize from this study that guilt is not an objective emotion, but experienced very differently person to person.

Many of those we have helped with guilt imagine a global 'guilt-o-meter' upon which everyone rates a score. Clearly, if they are feeling terribly guilty, they assume that they must be featuring high up on this global scale of unacceptability, when in fact their monitor is set to a completely different sensitivity from that of their neighbours. Accepting that you may have 'high guilt proneness' can prove very supportive to the CBT work we are going to engage in later in this book.

You can easily find a copy of the GASP questionnaire on the internet if you would like to score yourself. However, we would suggest that the very fact that you were reading this book indicates that you probably fall within the top 30–40% of people on the scale.

⇨ *Notes:*

_____

_____

_____

The father of lies

Our genetics, brains and upbringing are only part of the problem: there is another force at play. Christians believe in a conscious force of evil, often called Satan, and a spiritual battle in which we have a part to play. The writer to the Ephesians says that this fight is 'against the powers of this dark world and against the spiritual forces of evil' (Ephesians 6:12).

Notwithstanding the fact that God has won the victory, Satan does have real power. In overcoming guilt, we need to take this enemy seriously and recognize his tactics so that we can avoid being outwitted by him. Then, as Paul wrote to the Corinthians, we can say, 'We are not unaware of his schemes' (2 Corinthians 2:11).

Satan's first tactic is to sell us things that are wrong without telling us about the guilt that will come later. In *Precious Remedies against Satan's Devices*,[10] a Puritan called Thomas Brooks explains how Satan will 'bait our hook' with anything that we find desirable. His goal is for us to take the bait without seeing the hook. Once the hook is in our mouth, he reels us in to take us as his captive. These things then go on to make us feel guilty. To be sure, they are pleasurable for a short time (see Hebrews 11:25b), but they then turn very sour indeed.

Satan has two characteristics that are relevant to our discussion about guilt:

- Satan is called the 'father of lies' (John 8:44). He often distorts the truth in subtle ways that have catastrophic consequences. Where guilt is concerned, this can be convincing us of the goodness of bad things (as above) or convincing us of the badness of good things (like our consciences).
- Satan is called the 'accuser of our brothers and sisters' (Revelation 12:10). His accusations are often about whether we are good enough for God, whether we have committed some unforgivable sin, or that we have not lived up to God's calling. We can then be tempted to shy away from our true calling and lose the joy of our forgiveness.

To quote General Booth (the founder of the Salvation Army), 'The Devil should *not* have all the best tunes!' Booth used this as inspiration to start the brass bands we often hear playing carols at Christmas – in their day, they were at the cutting edge of popular music. His aim was to show that, while Satan might lie to us that all the fun is to be had 'over there', you could actually have plenty of fun with God 'over here' – and that that fun was more holistic, lasted longer and came guilt-free.

> Jenny had been a Christian for seven years. She had been converted at a summer camp, but had never felt as close to God since. For a while, her doctrines and church kept her faith firm, but as she grew older, she found more doubts and uncertainty creeping in.[11] She wanted to 'know' and to 'feel' as convinced as she had been when she had first come to faith. Her thoughts felt very sharp and accusatory.
>
> She felt far from God and struggled to believe that he was actually interested in her. By contrast, her new group of friends at the tennis club excited her, and the sport made her feel alive. She still believed, but now felt guilty that she doubted, guilty that she did not feel more certain, and even guilty about enjoying a game of tennis.

The 'lies' and 'accusations', of course, can come either from our own brains or the active work of Satan, or both – the key is discerning their source.

Occasionally, it seems that recurrent guilty thoughts are more self-attacking and that a specific evil origin should be considered. This can be the case if the accusation is specifically about our relationship with God or the nature of God; also,

if the thought is out of character for us and with no trigger
or cause. Spiritual guilt is very often diffuse and offers no clear
issue to repent of. Occult practices can sometimes open the
door to these experiences. If you have been involved with
the occult, we advise you to seek the advice of your pastor
and ask for spiritual help with this issue.[12]

Identifying thinking styles

Have you been to IKEA recently? Despite the warehouse
being a giant rectangular building, its interior has been
carefully designed to take you on a meandering journey that
makes perfect sense to the person looking to buy household
products. Relaxing music soothingly moves you along at a
reasonable pace, past kitchen, dining-room, study, bathroom
and bedroom furniture. However, if you happen to be in a
hurry, you may become frustrated by the pace and seek to
take one of the staff shortcuts that join different areas
together. Of course, whilst this makes your route faster, the
shopping experience IKEA has planned for you will no longer
make sense.

CBT tells us that our brains are a bit like the IKEA
warehouse. Information is sensibly stored, and yet at times
we use short cuts to help us process information more quickly.
Imagine, though, that taking any short cut in IKEA always
sent you back through the 'fitted kitchen' section. This would
quickly become frustrating and distressing.

People who struggle with false guilt likewise have unhelpful
short cuts for information processing that lead them directly
through the 'Guilt Department' far more frequently than
people without the same 'bias'. As a result, the person suffering
from false guilt is constantly making guilt associations within
their current experiences.

The good news is that these thinking styles can be changed, and so you will suffer with fewer inappropriate guilty thoughts. Right now though, we are just asking you to notice your thoughts and consider the possibility that your guilty feelings could be due to learned patterns of false guilt rather than a specific wrong you have committed.

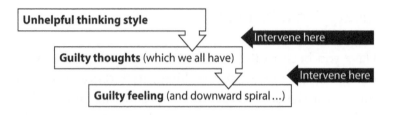

The table opposite (reproduced from a Five Areas® resource[13]) lists some 'negative thoughts' that come from things called 'thinking styles' (or 'biases'). This can happen when our mood is low, and so it becomes a vicious circle – the lower you are, the more you think in this style . . .

Do you recognize any of these styles and thoughts in yourself? Put a tick in the table if you have these thoughts often.

Do try to remember that all we are asking you to do here is spot patterns and problems, with a non-judgmental awareness. Just because you have been engaging in some of these patterns of thinking does not make you weak, deficient or foolish. Ironically, given the opportunity to help ourselves by becoming aware of areas in which we need to change, we can also create new things to feel guilty about.

As you review your list of 'areas for work', try to speak compassionately to yourself, recognizing that you have never willingly chosen a thinking style that may be unhelpful to you.

Unhelpful thinking style	Typical negative thoughts that go with it	☑
Bias against myself	I overlook my strengths I focus on my weaknesses I downplay my achievements I am my own worst critic	
Putting a negative slant on things	I see things through dark-tinted glasses I tend to focus on the negative in situations	
Having a gloomy view of the future	I make negative predictions about the future I predict that things will go wrong I predict that the very worst events will happen	
Negative view about how others see me	I mind-read what others think of me I often think that others don't like me/think badly of me	
Bearing all responsibility	I take the blame if things go wrong I feel responsible for whether everyone else has a good time I take unfair responsibility for things that are not my fault	
Making extreme statements/ rules	I use the words 'always', 'never' and 'typical' a lot, to summarize things I make myself a lot of 'must', 'should' 'ought' or 'got to' rules	
Jumping to conclusions	I move quickly to decisions on what is right or wrong I seem to 'know' what is going on intuitively I pick one thing and base my views on that	

Summary

It's not surprising that some people seem to hold on to guilt like a magnet – their brains are built that way. Most schools of psychology offer explanations of how guilt becomes embedded. It can also be seen on brain scans. You may rate highly on the 'GASP scale'. Additionally, Satan has a vested interest in seeing you weighed down by guilt and feeling 'accused'.

Many of our thoughts and feelings arise from our style of thinking, not from our actions. So we do not necessarily need to change what we are doing or not doing, but instead change the *way* we think – our thinking 'style'. Let us be compassionate, understanding and non-judgmental in the way we help ourselves to make future changes.

Exercises

Which psychological model (analytical, cognitive or behavioural) made most sense to you? Why?

_____

_____

_____

_____

_____

_____

Why is it significant that you can 'see' guilty thoughts on brain scans? How would you use this information when talking to someone who did not understand problematic guilt and why you struggle with it?

_____

_____

_____

_____

_____

_____

From the table on page 75, which three negative thinking styles are you most affected by?

1. _____

_____

2. _____

_____

3. _____

_____

Write an example of a guilty thought that goes with each
thinking style you noticed. Try to use your own words and
write them out in full.

1. _____

_____

_____

_____

2. _____

_____

_____

_____

3. _____

_____

_____

_____

For one of your thought styles (the one that causes you the
most trouble), write what response you might give to someone
else who struggled with this too.

- Thought:

_____

_____

_____

- Response:

_____

_____

_____

4. Guilt edged – a life tinged with badness

*Sadly, we do a much better job of making people feel guilty
than we do of delivering them from the guilt we create.
We need to confess this and change our ways.*
Tony Campolo[1]

Imagine Cedric, a Brazilian giant tortoise. He is primarily concerned with what is going on within his shell – whether he feels hungry, thirsty or sleepy. Yet, his external environment has a direct impact upon his experience of life within the shell. If the external world is warm and welcoming, he will extend his limbs and explore the garden confidently. However, if it is hostile or if he feels overwhelmed by responsibility, he will withdraw into his shell. What Cedric is not aware of is that withdrawal brings beliefs about the world and himself back into the shell with him.

We are rather like Cedric in that we tend to be concerned with our internal guilt. We generally believe that the origin of this feeling is within us and a direct result of our behaviour. Whilst this is correct for true guilt, false guilt is often generated by influences from within our external worlds. These typically challenging experiences lead us to withdraw and then generate guilty feelings as a way of making sense of what we have experienced.

In this chapter, we will be examining the role of our external worlds in generating guilty feelings. It is not possible for us to describe fully every environment that could generate false guilt here, and so this chapter will use five specific examples that relate to our roles, relationships, realities and religion. We suggest that you look at the general principles that we identify and then try to apply them to your own life experience.

Guilt we experience when we parent or lead (our roles)

Guilt, like charity, begins at home! Whilst writing *The Pregnancy Book* several years ago, I (Will) was repeatedly struck by the strength of guilt felt by new parents. Most parenting books and websites have a section dedicated to what is commonly termed in the US: 'Mommy guilt'. One popular site for new mums recounts:

> *Motherhood and Guilt seem to go hand in hand. Why is that? I am yet to meet a mother who has not had a conversation that starts with, 'I feel so guilty because . . .' As I discovered and explored in my own life, behind the guilt that I felt about being a mother, regardless of what it was about, there was a hidden 'should'. Something that I 'should' be doing other than what I was actually doing.*[2]

As parents, both Rob and I (alongside our respective wives!) can relate to the power of parental guilt. The reality is that a conscientious parent will at some point ask the inevitable question: 'Have I done enough for my child?' When our children were very young, we were filled with insecurities and therefore measured ourselves against the standards of those who made parenting look easy.

Now, a few years on and as more experienced and mature parents (but still with much to learn, of course), we realize that the angelic-looking child in the playground is very often terrorizing his family at home! But it can still be hard. We still make comparisons; we still beat ourselves up and jump to the worst conclusions. These beliefs rarely bear any relationship to our genuine qualities as parents, but they say far more about how we feel about our parenting.

Psychology Today[3] listed the things parents feel most guilty about. Here are their top ten:

I wasn't there enough.
I didn't listen.
I was too focused on the house and work.
I wasn't affectionate enough.
I was critical.
I shouted, smacked and blamed.
I was a bad role model.
I didn't take the time to understand my children.
I wasn't consistent.
I pushed too hard.

Five ways to manage parenting guilt (or responsibility-based guilt)

1. Recognize that being responsible for your child (or other people's welfare) does not require you to be a perfect parent (or leader), but just 'good enough'.
2. You are the right person for the role of parent (or leader), even when there are other people who have skills that are more developed than yours.

3. Discuss how feelings of deficiency, or comparison-making, can generate feelings of guilt with other parents (or comparable colleagues).
4. Spend time outside of your role (take a break) for a couple of hours or so each week to remind yourself that you are also a child who needs care and nurture.
5. Spend time in worship, focusing on the strength and provision of God. Pray that you will recognize his calling and equipping for your current role or responsibility.

Parenting guilt is a very powerful manifestation of false guilt that is not just specific to parents. Similar forms of guilt are felt by people in all sorts of positions of responsibility within society. If you are a carer, a business leader, a teacher, a team leader or in any number of other positions, the sense that you are deficient or 'not good enough' will lead to guilty feelings. Of course, as with all 'false guilt', these feelings are false. They are often generated because you care too much, not because you don't care enough. The five principles above should help you whether or not you are a parent.

Guilt we experience because of how we were parented (our relationships)

Feeling guilty *as* a parent (or responsible person) is very different from having been parented *by* guilt, what some psychologists call 'guilt induction'.

> [Guilt induction is] the degree to which the parent achieved goals or attempted to control or change the behaviour or opinions of

the child by means of contingent complaints, manipulation, or revealing needs or wants in a whiny and blaming manner. These expressions convey the sense that *the parent's life is made worse by something the child does* (e.g. the message is given that if the child does not behave as requested, the parent will be distressed.[4] (emphasis added)

Unfortunately, guilt is a very efficient means of control, and parents who struggle with being assertive may fall into the trap of using it to keep the peace at home. There are of course other ways to induce guilt, and we can also start to feel guilty later in life. But many who struggle with guilt today report that they were made to feel guilty when they were young.

However, very few parents set out to use guilt as a means of parenting; nearly all fall into the trap of expressing their frustration through their mood. These moods quickly provoke responses and concerns from their children who notice when mummy goes quiet on them, and so they are then easily manipulated into acceptable behaviours. As I relayed the details of this chapter to a friend of mine, she recounted how, when misbehaving as a child, her mother would say, 'You're only doing that because you want mummy to die.' It doesn't get much more guilt-inducing than that.

A recent study from the University of Jyväskylä, Finland showed that 'when parents used higher levels of guilt-inducing parenting on certain days, this was evident as atypically high levels of distress and anger among children still on the next day'.[5] The impact of this distress over time is discussed by another study that concludes: 'Higher levels of parental guilt induction were related to higher levels of child internalising problems.'[6]

Children who have grown up in a perpetual state of distress move from *experiencing* problems into believing that they *are* the problem. The outworking of a parenting guilt culture in the home is that the child tends to self-blame. This will lead them to overestimate their responsibility for events outside of their control and to punish themselves with exaggerated feelings of guilt. It is worth mentioning here that marital breakdowns very often inadvertently leave children believing that they are partially responsible, and they may therefore carry a huge burden of false guilt.

Guilt-inducing parenting styles can lead people to behave in the same way years later. This does not make it OK, but does explain why a family guilt culture can become a generational problem. Have you noticed this in your own family perhaps?

Danny's not sure exactly, but he has a hunch that his mum may have been depressed when he was small. He remembers Dad telling him to be quiet, 'coz Mum was sad, or tired' or something. His older brother just didn't seem to care, was always slamming doors and storming off, but Danny was Mummy's 'kind helper'. If Mummy was crying, it was Danny who brought her a cushion or a tissue or his favourite storybook.

Danny prayed a lot for his family. He wasn't sure if it was normal to pray that much, but he didn't care. He thought that maybe something bad was going to happen at home and that perhaps it would be his fault, especially if he didn't pray right or for long enough or say 'Amen' earnestly enough.

When Danny took his brother's football without asking, there was a real 'blow up'. Dad was cross, Mum was crying and his brother stormed off. For a couple of hours no-one knew where Danny's brother was. Mum said, 'She would never forgive Danny if anything bad had happened.' After a while, everything seemed normal again. Apart from the guilt.

Danny felt bad most of the time. He worried a lot about things that might go wrong and he wasn't certain that bad things that other people had done weren't his fault in some strange, almost 'magical', way. If he was ever asked if he had done something, he always confessed straight away, even if he wasn't sure it really was his fault. After all, he would much rather take whatever punishment was going than suffer under the weight of the guilt and uncertainty he would feel if he denied it.

Danny's adult life and relationships were all affected by his proneness to guilt. On the outside, he was successful and well liked (because he never offended anyone). What people didn't know, however, was how much he struggled with low feelings, self-doubt and exaggerated guilt. No matter how many times he prayed or spoke to his pastor about it, guilt for something or other would always creep back into the picture.

Danny's story is a good example of the potential impact of a family 'guilt-culture', one where parenting through guilt induction was commonplace. Danny's brother was most likely responding to the same parenting as Danny, but used avoidance and anger to defend himself against absorbing it.

You may think Danny's story is an exaggerated illustration. However, it is actually an amalgamation of a 'toned-down' real-life testimony I have heard. Because of the insecurity and doubt that family guilt cultures create, it is very rare to capture a glimpse of what many people spend their whole life trying to hide. Of course, the experience of 'guilt-induction' parenting is just one example of a whole range of settings in which false guilt can be used as a means of relational control. Marriages, sibling relationships and even social friendships all have the propensity to use guilt in a destructive and controlling manner.

Exercises

Spend some time reflecting quietly on your experience of guilt within your immediate family.

- Try to avoid laying blame, but remain compassionate towards both yourself and other family members.
- If you feel that it may be helpful and appropriate, seek to have a conversation with a sibling about their experience of familial guilt. Again, try to remain impartial and remember that others may have quite different memories of childhood from your own.

⇨ Make any notes here:

_____

_____

_____

Learning cultures and guilt (our realities)

You might not necessarily associate schools, universities or colleges with guilt. When we consider their emotional value, it tends to be within more simplistic categories, such as success-versus-failure or popularity-versus-isolation. However, many 'learning cultures' inadvertently employ guilt-induction teaching styles as a means of enforcing standards, maintaining discipline and motivating reluctant students.

In many school settings, particularly those that are privately funded, there is a convergence of familial and institutional guilt. It is this convergence of two different sources of guilt that has the most detrimental long-term effect. Having previously been a schoolteacher, I (Will) sense some internal conflict in writing this. I am aware that, as a teacher, you have a responsibility to enable your pupils to achieve their full potential. In order to do this, they often have to gather an appreciation of the costs and privileges of education, as well as their own unmet potential, all of which generates guilt.

Of course, the vast majority of students navigate the guilt used to motivate them through education without many problems. For others, the guilt of failing to meet the expect-ations of teachers and parents (not to mention any fees involved) can set the pattern for ongoing problems.

A psychotherapist called Carl Jung said that many insti-tutions (particularly the places where we learn) become like artificial 'Mothers'[7] to us, and when we look to them for love, we are disappointed. We then experience the guilt of being a disappointment, of failing to reach expectations and of meeting all of 'her' demands and requirements.[8]

Athalia was a very bright second-generation British Indian Christian, living in Reading UK. Neither of her grandparents had had any formal education when they had moved to the UK, and her own parents had worked extremely hard to build up a profitable retail business from scratch. Athalia's natural aptitude had been noticed in primary school, and she had been offered a partial scholarship to a private girls' day school.

Athalia's parents made huge sacrifices for her extra tutoring and subsequent partial school fees. Her mother constantly reminded her, 'What a blessed girl you are to have such privileges.' Athalia was often paraded around at family gatherings as their great success story and the fulfilment of their struggle from poverty to prosperity. And Athalia's school experience was not vastly different from her home life. She was upheld as a model student and received various prizes and privileges, all of which fuelled the already high levels of self-expectation that she carried.

Unsurprisingly, as the pressures of school exams loomed, Athalia's anxiety, combined with the expectations of her family, quickly morphed into guilt and self-recrimination. A couple of B grades completely destroyed the joy of her many A grades. Athalia began to internalize her guilt to the extent that it simply became an amorphous sense of discomfort that bore little relationship to any real events.

Athalia's journey with familial guilt wasn't resolved until she did a psychiatric placement as an undergraduate medical student at Cambridge University. Through a gentle conversation with her tutor, she began to realize that she had a complex and lifelong problem with false guilt, but that it could now be addressed and changed. Subsequent work with a psychotherapist explored her family interactions and early school life. This changed her perspective, and she was able to move away from compulsive confessions and self-recrimination. This change revolutionized her daily life and restored her damaged self-confidence.

A consumer society and guilt (our realities)

So far, we have explored both the family and learning environments as places that can have a strong influence on the development of false guilt. Although less pronounced, it would be a mistake not to mention the power of Western society in our cycles of false guilt.[9]

I live in London and over the past ten years I have seen an explosion of advertising hoardings along my route into the city. London, like many other great cities, is a centre for business, and consumers of one kind or another support its success. From this interaction, we get the title 'consumerism': the act of fuelling the hunger within the purchaser for the goods of the manufacturer. Consumerism is generally frowned upon in the Christian world; however, that doesn't mean it doesn't exist within our churches. Consumerism is something that we cannot get away from in a market economy; whether you agree with it or not, economic stability and national wealth are based upon this transaction.

Life in our society is guilt edged because of the important role guilt plays within consumerism. You may well have heard the term 'consumer guilt', but the guilt we experience in our culture is far more diffuse than just that held within the minds of those who make excessive and lavish purchases. It is not just those who buy the 'boys' toy' who feel it – there can be guilt over whether you have bought the *right* toy, from the *right* brand, at the *right* price. Advertising in consumer cultures is typically loaded to exploit the strong desire within humanity for group acceptance. It is said that the only thing that all humans truly crave is acceptance and the only thing they truly fear is rejection.

Advertising says that if you buy X, Y or Z, then you will be acceptable, increasing a person's hope of inclusion in, or admiration from, the group. From this principle, we see a capitalist's dream: the birth of a 'trend', where the whole group seeks to demonstrate their identity through buying a shared product. Dare you buy a lesser model . . . ?

The challenges of a consumer society can sound so simple when explained in this way. However, the true picture is complicated by an infinite number of different groups with different rules for inclusion and exclusion. Perhaps one day I will fulfil a lifelong ambition to ride a motorbike and be included in a biker group. My sense of deficiency and exclusion as a people-carrier driver with biscuit crumbs between the seats will finally be behind me!

When purchasing a bike, I will need to navigate which one to buy: chopper, moped or super-bike.[10] If I purchase the chopper, I will need to buy clothes that reflect my desire for inclusion in a Chopper Bike Club. Having done so, I will have excluded myself from the other groups, as well as received the scorn of the environmentalists who classify my sort of bike as a crime against the climate. I may then offend the road safety directive by taking my son to school on the back, and be scorned by other parents for having a desperate mid-life crisis. At the end of the day, I may feel so guilty that I end up taking the bike back to the shop and buying a family-sized car with low emissions and great fuel economy (and space for crumbs).

The guilt we get from our society is a good example of the power of false guilt. It is not something that we can overcome, but by being aware of it, we can amend our responses and be far more flexible and generous. If you can, laugh at yourself too.

A church divided by guilt (our religion)

The church, like society, can be heavily stratified on the basis of false guilt. Typically, ex-offenders and people with 'colourful pasts' are encouraged to speak up and 'share their testimony', but rarely do they progress through the guilt divide into leadership or responsibility. Despite the gospel being 'for

sinners', and St Paul referencing himself as 'the worst
of sinners' (1 Timothy 1:16), many church families struggle
to empower reformed 'sinners' in the ministry of the church.

In places, the church can be worse than society, as the
divorcee, bankrupt person or individual who has struggled with
their sexuality feels permanently and publicly stained. Here,
the equality we share before God has become distorted by a
very human perception of worthiness. It is important to clarify
that 'God's holiness' and 'human worthiness' are very different
virtues. Any sense in which the church stratifies the spiritual
virtue of its members will fuel a guilt-laden culture where every
individual ultimately takes on the mantle of, 'not good enough'.

Ian knew he came from the wrong side of the tracks. His
family were notorious in the small market town where
he lived, and people genuinely feared him and his
brothers. Although he had experienced only minor
'brushes' with the law, he had a long history of anti-social
behaviour, drug use and petty crime. Ian's conversion
came as more of a shock to himself than it had done to
the rest of his family.

One afternoon in the local park, he had listened in to
an Irish minister preaching to his congregation as part
of a week-long mission. Ian returned every day, hearing
the man speak about sin and forgiveness. At the end of the
week, with tears streaming down his cheeks, the thirty-
year-old came forward to receive Jesus for himself.

Over the subsequent months, Ian became something
of a Christian celebrity, giving his testimony at public
meetings and being warmly applauded by members of
the church. He even spoke on local radio. However, a
few years later, Ian was really struggling to integrate into

> the church family. Despite being very loved and supported
> by the pastor and many individuals in the church, he
> could not shake off the sense that he was perceived to be
> inappropriate for more than practical-service roles.
>
> He struggled with persistent guilt about the past and,
> despite a wholesale lifestyle change, felt he could not
> convince the church to trust him. Those chosen for
> leadership did not necessarily have any more faith or
> spiritual maturity than he did; they just had a less dramatic
> life story.

Ian's story highlights the tension between the perfection of
God's unconditional love and the struggle of conditional
human love. The reality is that, whilst people are worshipping
together on earth, no congregation is going to be free from
the pitfalls of human judgment. Jesus himself spoke out
against a religious culture that propagated false guilt and
excluded people on the basis of their backgrounds, education
or social standing. If we are to follow his example, we need
to become aware of our own propensity to generate false
guilt, as well as be victims of it.

Summary

In this chapter, we have identified four broad areas of life in
which we can experience inappropriate feelings of guilt: our
roles (as parents or leaders), our relationships (including
parenting style), our realities (as recipients of education and
people in a consumer society) and our religion (as members
of a still-learning church).

In the following chapters, we are going to explore ways in
which these cycles of false guilt can be broken and undone.

Exercises

Write a school report for yourself aged between ten and thirteen, using the following headings as a guide:

1. Dealing with familial and school expectations

   _____

   _____

2. Meeting your potential

   _____

   _____

3. Understanding what is your/others' responsibility

   _____

   _____

4. Experiencing/managing false guilt

   _____

   _____

What is your overall impression of your personal journey with false guilt, in your roles, relationships, realities and your religion?

_____

_____

How has your experience informed your tendency to be judgmental of yourself or others?

_____

_____

Imagine a close friend came to you, wracked with false guilt. What would you point out from this chapter to give them a more realistic perspective?

_____

_____

5. A guilty conscience – spotting false-guilt traps

For the sadness that is used by God
brings a change of heart that leads to salvation –
and there is no regret in that!
But sadness that is merely human causes death.
2 Corinthians 7:10 GNT

'It *must* be bad . . .'

Trusting your own feelings has become something of a virtue in the twenty-first century. We are told by very successful people that following their instincts led to their highest achievements. Donald Trump's number-one tip for success is: 'Trust your gut!' Even in the church, we consider our feelings to be a good marker of our spiritual condition. Every month, I (Will) counsel lots of people and very often the first question I ask them is: 'How are you feeling?' Because they *feel* bad, they assume they must have *done* something bad. From their response and their assumption of sin, we begin our work of discussion, counsel and prayer.

⇨ Assumption: feeling EQUALS fact

Imagine now that the powerful 'feeling' of guilt that plagues you may be a 'mental event' that has no foundation in the reality of your actions. Again, we are not talking here about 'true guilt' that has been dealt with; we are talking about the strong sense of guilt that suddenly and often unexpectedly pounces on you without provocation. Imagine then, if that were the case, the months of anguish you have been experiencing; all of the activities you have undertaken to assuage your guilt would actually have provided no benefit at all. It has just been a 'feeling' that you have been chasing.

⇨ Alternative belief: feeling DOES NOT EQUAL fact

Can we sow the seed of uncertainty in your mind, that the 'feeling' you experience should not automatically be presumed to point to a truth? It can be helpful just to consider the alternative – and often you will be able to say it is *more likely than not* that something else is going on.

In 2005, when I (Will) was suffering from overwhelming anxiety following the London bombings, I was suddenly plagued by a terrifying wave of guilty feelings and memories. At the time, I was completely unaware of the psychological link between anxiety / depression and guilt. As a result, I found myself reliving some very painful experiences. I made lots of confessions to my poor wife of things that most other people would think were mere trifles as well as some things which were genuinely sinful. I even phoned up old friends to try to make apologies for things I thought I had done wrong years ago!

Interestingly, as soon as my anxiety / depression lifted, those long-forgiven issues became just memories again and lost their emotional power. Insight returned!

Professor Paul Gilbert says, 'As people become more depressed, they can also feel more guilty. They may start to focus and dwell on things that they have done or not done that they think have harmed others.'[1] This is a great example of how false guilt can masquerade as true guilt, depending on our particular emotional state.

Of course, if you struggle badly with false guilt, you will not believe this suggestion. Even now, you will most probably be thinking of several concrete events that you feel guilty about in order to prove that this potential 'disclaimer' does not apply to you. For now, can we just encourage you to think of it like a 'hypothesis' – something we are going to check out together?

False-guilt traps

There are things that keep false guilt going, mostly things that you do because you think and 'feel' that they will help, and as such you are doing your best. Most people who struggle with guilt do some or all of them.

This does not mean you are foolish. However, especially with hindsight, it is clear that they do not help as much as you may wish or think. In fact, they provide a degree of reassurance, like checking you have locked the front door. So, they are valued as helpful and become part of a vicious circle keeping false guilt going. You believe them more and more.

Everybody has relatively regular experience of irrational doubt and subsequent checking behaviour. Perhaps in the house at night, you hear a noise. Your rational mind knows that this sound most probably came from the neighbour's cat or a party-goer walking home. However, the 'feelings'-orientated part of you is uncomfortable,

> and therefore, despite its futility, you get out of bed and go downstairs and check that the doors are locked and there isn't an intruder. Once you 'feel right', you are able to accept what your rational mind had been telling you and return to bed.

Our 'false-guilt hypothesis' suggests that those who struggle with false guilt operate in a very similar way. For them, a feeling of guilt provokes a virtual journey 'downstairs' into the memory banks, checking the vaults for historic moral failures or potential new and previously unseen moral intruders. The combination of strong guilty feelings and persistent uncertainty means that it can take a very long time indeed to be able to 'return to bed' and feel at peace.

The more you seek relief from 'false guilt' and get some temporary respite, the more convinced you will become of your actual guilt and the more 'false-guilt events' you will experience. I asked a godly seventy-year-old friend if she ever felt guilt without clear reason. She said, 'I feel guilt all of the time. I think I have felt guilty my whole life.' By anyone's standards, she is an outstanding example of faith and holiness, and she also knows that God has forgiven her true guilt. I hope her testimony alone is enough to convince you that false guilt is very real and that it doesn't fade without taking the correct steps to address it. Her determined and best efforts had failed.

We call these activities 'false-guilt traps', and it is essential that you don't dismiss them as meaningless little rituals that make you feel better. 'False-guilt traps' actually reinforce the problem of false guilt, and whilst they can give short-term relief from the pain of a guilty and doubt-filled conscience, they ultimately reinforce the false belief. Here are some common traps.

1. The search

Another friend of mine smells bonfires when she is stressed. This slightly unusual stress response used to cause her a high level of anxiety, but now it provides a useful early-warning sign that she needs to moderate her activity to regain her sense of peace. Imagine, rather than linking this experience to stress, she actually made the more obvious connection to fire. How many fire alarms would have been pulled? How many buildings evacuated? How long do you think it would take before she realized that this was a 'mental event' and not an indication of an external reality? When we are worried, we try to check things out and err on the side of caution.

The first and most universal response to 'false guilt' is the initiation of a checking behaviour we call 'the search'. In a similar way to smelling a bonfire, a person experiences the 'smell' of false guilt. This is a combination of doubt, anguish and fear. In its initial form, it is often an almost physical sensation that appears apparently out of the blue – what the old hymn writers called a 'guilty stain' that seems to spread before your eyes.

Any trigger can be the stimulus, such as a disturbing news report or an odd look from a colleague. However, people who suffer from excessive guilt problems are typically conscientious, moral, compassionate and empathetic. Hence, they also have a tendency to review what they have done and find their own internal triggers. The Christian call to holiness can double this, as there is an extra motivation to search and an extra concern if you are found wanting. As a result, the slightest smell of guilt sends Christians on 'the search' to clarify the threat. It surely makes sense that if you can 'smell' guilt, there must be something there to create that 'smell'; 'there's no smoke without fire' and all that. The trouble is that you can actually search for a fire physically, but how can you accurately search for the source of guilt?

The result of 'the search' is not that there is nothing to feel bad about; instead it always finds something worthy of the feeling. As we are aware from chapter 2, we have all done things for which we appropriately feel 'true guilt'. The maddening quality of false guilt is that it will take all of your resolved true guilt and reignite it to answer the most pressing question of the moment: 'Why do I feel so bad?'

We all have genuine reasons to feel ashamed of our behaviour, but thanks to God's forgiveness, we can leave them in the past. However, it seems to make more sense for the brain to identify a relationship breakdown from fifteen years ago as the source of the current 'guilt smell' than it does for the brain to concede that there just isn't anything behind these terrible feelings. In this way, 'the search' answers the immediate question with a false positive and by the same token reaffirms that you are a bad person who deserves to be punished by those guilty feelings. This seems morally more consistent (we do know we are sinners, after all . . .), rather than trying to live as a hypocrite. This reaffirmation of your assumed guilt means that you are even more susceptible to believe the next guilt event without even questioning it.

2. Escape and avoidance

Psychologists describe the activities that we undertake to escape painful feelings as 'safety behaviours'. These offer some short-term relief from the emotional pain that an individual may be experiencing. In the long term, however, these behaviours themselves become problematic and impinge on a person's quality of life or freedom. False guilt provokes some very specific 'safety behaviours' that offer this short-term relief but ultimately further fuel emotional suffering.

In the 1994 Disney animated classic, *The Lion King*, the lion cub Simba is falsely blamed for the death of his father Mufasa. The young cub is not aware that his evil uncle Scar had orchestrated this murder to take the throne for himself. Simba is so burdened by false guilt that he places himself into exile, separating himself from the pride and casting aside his role and vision as the rightful heir.

Humans, like lions, have a healthy and natural aversion to pain, both physical and emotional. As a result, it is unusual for the person plagued by intense feelings of guilt to stay with these feelings for long. The most basic way to try to avoid guilt is to avoid any triggers. People can become reclusive, avoid friendships and not do the things they would like to do. They can also think this protects their 'smell' or 'stain' of guilt from affecting others.

Frankly, avoidance is rarely possible, as most people have to engage with others to some degree. So, the second most basic way to reduce guilt is to escape from situations when it gets too bad. Examples of this include leaving church early before Communion, making casual friends but ending the friendship before things deepen, or withdrawing abruptly from a project because you think you will mess it up.

Like avoidance, repeated escapes are not possible all that often, so people may use some of the more subtle safety behaviours below. Just like escape and avoidance, they are not really solutions because, though they may lessen your anxiety a small amount, they keep it ticking along and stop you from learning what is really going on.

3. Compulsive confession

James 5:16 says, 'Confess your sins to each other and pray for each other so that you may be healed. The prayer of a righteous person is powerful and effective.' Not only is confession biblical; it also provides almost instant emotional benefits. When our consciences are truly provoked, what greater healing can we receive than that of humbly confessing our error and asking for forgiveness? Confession is a gift from God and something that I see bringing release and healing to hundreds of people every year. It is a great response to true guilt.

It is unsurprising, given that most people with guilt problems are struggling to differentiate between true and false types, that confession is also employed as a way for people to escape the feelings of false guilt.

I spoke to a leader of a suburban church who was exhausted by an elderly woman who had started knocking on his door with alarming frequency. Every time, she was tearful and wracked with guilt. As was his tradition, this priest felt compelled to hear her confession and confirm the absolution of her sins. Yet, just a day or so later, she would come back in exactly the same state to recount some newly recalled sin from her past. It was clear that this woman's life was actually being overtaken by the desire to escape from false guilt and that she was using compulsive confession to do this.

There are three vital things to know about compulsive confession that will help you spot it when it is going on and enable you to start acting in different ways:

1. Compulsive confession is always a response to the painful feelings of false guilt rather than the reality of a true-guilt issue. As a result, it will always be seeking to remove the guilty feelings around a sin that has been

confessed before (usually several times). There is no
need for repeated confession. Isaiah 43:25 says,

> I, even I, am he who blots out
>> your transgressions, for my own sake,
>> and remembers your sins no more.

This verse is absolutely clear that God both removes
and forgets confessed sin. You can see, then, that it is
problematic to believe that you can make God
remember a sin that he has already removed from you
and chosen to forget.

2. Compulsive confession tends to become very legalistic
   and often presupposes that every single sin ever
   committed must be consciously thought of and
   confessed if it is to be forgiven. This is contrary to the
   nature of God who is full of grace and love. What is
   essential is not a formula, but the forgiving nature of
   God. It is also important to note that God knows us
   completely and forgives us completely when we come
   to him in the *spirit* of confession, not *knowingly* holding
   anything back. I am sure you have had the experience
   of suddenly realizing you have been doing something
   wrong for years, but only recently has God begun to
   draw your attention to it – how could you have
   confessed this sin that you did not know existed?

3. Compulsive confession is ultimately seeking concrete
   feelings of forgiveness. Being a Christian is to respond to
   God's rescue plan, what Jesus did for us on the cross, and
   to enter into friendship with him. If we are looking to
   find validation for this in our own feelings, we will be
   disappointed. The 'freedom feeling' of forgiveness is
   rarely retained constantly or indefinitely. However, it is

the truth of God's forgiveness that is of ultimate importance, not the feeling of freedom. If a person is *feeling* doubt and guilt, the likelihood is that they are dealing with a false-guilt issue and should flatly refuse the urge to make a new confession, but instead sit with the feelings long enough for them to dissipate on their own, which they will do if they are not reinforced. John Wesley, the eighteenth-century preacher, commented, 'This is properly termed a scrupulous conscience, and it is highly expedient to yield to it as little as possible, rather it is a matter of prayer that you may be delivered from the sore evil and may recover a sound mind.'[2]

Compulsive confession is a very addictive habit and it can be very destructive. Through the work of the Mind and Soul Foundation (see p. 196), we are aware of people who have damaged their relationships through the compulsion to confess every single negative thought. We have even come across people who have made false confessions to the police because they have become so riddled with doubt and guilt. This points to the reality that compulsive confession for false guilt damages our self-esteem, brings confusion over our responsibilities and makes us prone to further false guilt.

4. Rumination

If you cannot confess your way out of the pain of a falsely guilty conscience, perhaps you can just think your way out of it?

⇨ **Rumination** is defined on Wikipedia as 'the compulsively focused attention on the symptoms of one's distress, and on its possible causes and consequences, as opposed to its solutions. Rumination is similar to worry except rumination

> focuses on bad feelings and experiences from the past,
> whereas worry is concerned with potential bad events in
> the future. Both rumination and worry are associated with
> anxiety and other negative emotional states.'[3]

Most people who struggle with false guilt will have a degree
of insight that their emotions do not match the facts, and so
confession to another person seems far too exposing. They
fear the embarrassment of being told that their confession is
unnecessary, and, more significantly, fear being told that it *is*
necessary! So instead, they ruminate.

Their escape is centred upon 'focusing on bad feelings and
experiences from the past' and the hope that this will locate
something that can be dealt with. The rumination that they
undertake is largely to pick through the memories of their
troubling ideas to try to discredit them by rationalizing them
or blame-sharing. But because false guilt latches on to a stream
of often distant and blurred memories or events, this is never
going to be very effective or result in any clarity. In fact, there
is a real danger of doubting what actually occurred, leaving
you in a worse place than before.

Emily was an apparently confident woman, working for
a marketing company within a competitive office. The
stress and pressure of the workplace were already having
an impact upon her sleep, but rather than becoming
angry or withdrawn, she just felt more sensitive, welling
up when anyone said a kind word to her or whilst
watching innocuous TV programmes.

Emily had been fighting for a promotion for several
years, and when at last she was told she had become a
section manager, she was delighted. However, it quickly

became clear that a close colleague had gone for the same post and had been rejected. She was instantly hostile towards Emily and insinuated that she was a heartless bully who had played a dirty game to gain the promotion.

Initially, Emily was furious, but this quickly turned into doubt and guilt. She began ruminating over her behaviour in the office, asking incessant questions about whether there wasn't some truth in her colleague's accusations. Her thoughts seemed to be on a roller-coaster through her memory banks, pulling out a litany of her 'greatest worst hits': a bullying incident at school, an angry tiff with a friend, a falling out with a parent. Before long, Emily felt wracked with guilt but also filled with doubt. She could not stop going over all of these events, rationally certain that they did not add up to confirmation that she was a hostile bully, yet still left with a sense of foreboding and badness.

Emily's self-confidence was badly depleted and she began to feel quite depressed. The more she tried to prove to herself that her colleague's accusation was false, the more guilt and doubt she felt. Whilst she knew she was desperately over-thinking, Emily felt almost compelled to ruminate; she just couldn't let it go.

Rumination is like giving someone a metal detector and sending them off to a scrap heap. The person wracked with false guilt will begin ruminating and, like Emily, they will believe that the process of 'thinking things over' will help them disprove what they fear. But rumination does exactly the opposite. Instead of disproving their guilt, it inevitably finds everything (the scrap) that would make one feel guilty and nothing that will prove them innocent. In a way, it is like 'the search' all over again. It can even invent evidence from scratch.

The other trouble with rumination is that it reinforces unhelpful thinking styles and distorts them further. When Emily set out to prove she was a good person, her thinking quickly became very black and white: she thought she was either guilty of bad behaviour and therefore a nasty person, or she was innocent of bad behaviour and was a nice person. The truth of course is that she was a complex mixture of the two – a forgiven sinner who will continue to sin until heaven, but growing in holiness! Rumination does not easily accept ambiguity, as it wants absolute certainty. As a result, rumination becomes a compulsion which won't be resolved.

When a person uses rumination regularly, they establish strong themes of concern to which they become hyper-vigilant. To take the metal detector idea a step further, hyper-vigilance is like programming the machine to be sensitive only to particular frequencies. In this way, the detector will beep only when it is held over steel or brass or gold. Many people who are suffering from false guilt will respond to any clues in conversation, environments or the media that link to their 'guilt-frequency'. This, in turn, triggers a wave of anxiety, followed by strong guilt that restarts the cycle of rumination all over again.

> Luke had lost control at school. Another boy in his year had made a joke about his mum being 'good looking'. Unbeknown to this other boy, Luke's parents were having marriage difficulties, and Luke was very unsettled and angry about what was going on at home. A fight broke out, and all of Luke's rage was channelled through one

or two punches. Subsequent suspension from school and the ultimate divorce of his parents left Luke riddled with guilt and shame. He felt that he had further compounded their problems and was partly responsible for the divorce.

As a young adult, Luke continued to be wracked with guilt. Despite the fight being a 'schoolboy' incident, any reference to 'assault' in any news report made his blood run cold, and he began replaying what had happened over and over in his mind. Now that he was older it felt far worse – he judged his teenage behaviour by adult standards. He must have been a bully; he was unprovoked. No matter how hard he tried to escape by thinking it through rationally, Luke felt terrible.

It wasn't just the fight that dominated Luke's mind; his relationships were also affected. Luke felt terrified that if he made any mistakes in the relationship or behaved badly in any way, he was sure to be abandoned. The more he checked his conduct, the more insecure he became. His constant quest for reassurance began to damage relationships, and Luke felt powerless to change his behaviour. Rumination became a regular and exhausting cycle of guilt induction, reassurance, seeking rumination and fleeting moments of peace.

5. Perfectionism

Earlier, we discussed compulsive confession as an attempt to assuage powerful guilty feelings. Perfectionism, however, is a class A drug to those who suffer with false guilt. What is more, few places (including churches and businesses) dissuade their members from its use! Stoeber and Childs argue, 'Perfectionism is a personality trait characterized by a person's striving for flawlessness and setting excessively high performance standards, accompanied by overly critical self-evaluations and concerns regarding others' evaluations.'[4] When you read their definition plainly, you can see just how anti-grace perfectionism is, and yet you can also see how the gospel of perfectionism has taken root in our churches.

Matthew 5:8 is clearly a stumbling block for many Christians who interpret the instruction: 'Be perfect . . . as your heavenly Father is perfect' as validation for their perfectionism. Instead the Greek word used for perfection, *teleioi*, also means 'complete'. Since we find our completion in Christ who restores us from our sinful deficiency, it is not hard to see the intended meaning of the verse. It is obviously foolish to suggest that Jesus was implying that the sort of perfection the law required was attainable through human effort. After all, Romans 3:10 states clearly, 'As it is written: "There is no-one righteous, not even one." ' The pursuit of holiness begins not in our righteous acts, but in our confessional hearts.

Ultimately, unless we see perfectionism for the enemy of grace that it really is, we will both suffer under its burden and be diminished in our experience of the complete love of God. Arianna Walker of Mercy Ministries UK says, 'Perfectionism steals the opportunity for you to ever feel the grace of God in your life.'[5] Grace more than any other virtue is the antidote to guilt and perfectionism.

Perfectionism grows up in people who have become intolerant of pain. They literally say to themselves, 'My life is agony because of guilt. I cannot possibly deal with any more pain, so I just have to get everything right from now on.' The logic of this sentiment is perfectly clear, but so is its abject impossibility. The motivation, however, is incredibly strong. Professor Stephen Phillipson says, 'There are powerful cognitive elements at work – their belief that their self-worth is at stake and that their value as a human being depends on their response to the particular situation they are facing.'[6]

> Sarah was from a large Christian family. Her home was a bustle of life and warmth, filled with seven children of whom Sarah was the second eldest. She had absolutely no idea where her guilty feelings originated from and could not recall any event that would warrant these bad feelings.
>
> Her parents constantly reaffirmed her 'goodness and kindness' in the way she looked after her younger siblings, but all this did was to make Sarah feel more fraudulent and therefore more guilty. She would look in the mirror and see an impostor whom she believed no-one really knew. Her ruminations centred upon her being 'found out' and expelled from the family she loved so much.
>
> As a result, Sarah became increasingly perfectionistic. She worked tirelessly to avoid criticism, became scrupulous about her Christian faith and was incessantly kind and good to her family. Of course, this only served to reinforce the belief her family had about her being 'perfect' and her own belief that she was an 'impostor', unknown by the people she loved the most. Over time, Sarah became exhausted and anxious, until finally she disclosed her true feelings to her school counsellor.

People who struggle with perfectionism have high standards, because they believe great things are at stake. These things do exist, to be sure, but they overemphasize the link between their actions and these things happening. Ultimately, as Anne Wilson Schaef says, 'Perfectionism is self-abuse of the highest order.'[7] If you struggle with perfectionism, you may identify with some of these things. Tick if the answer is 'yes'.

If I lower my standards, then:

- I will slip completely ☐
- I will become lazy ☐
- Others will think I am lazy ☐
- Others will not praise me ☐
- I will lose something I value (such as a job) ☐
- I will not progress ☐
- I will be average (and anonymous) ☐

Do you go one step further and think any of these things? If I lower my standards, then:

- People will die ☐
- People will not get saved ☐
- I will let God down ☐

We do not have sufficient space in this book to deal with people who really struggle with perfectionism. Such people will find many of the techniques in the rest of this book helpful, but you will also need a book that deals specifically with perfectionism. We would recommend *Overcoming Perfectionism* by Professor Ros Shafran and others.[8] This is not a Christian book, but you can read it alongside this one.

6. Punishment

'The Christian healing model' is established on the principle of 'substitution', where a 'divine exchange' takes place:

> He [Jesus] was pierced for our transgressions,
>   he was crushed for our iniquities;

the punishment that brought us peace was on him,
    and by his wounds we are healed.
(Isaiah 53:5)

One way of understanding God's grace is to see it as an acronym: G.R.A.C.E. – God's Riches (for me) At Christ's Expense.

Before he went to the cross, Jesus asked, 'If it is possible, may this cup [of suffering] be taken from me' (Matthew 26:39) – not because he wanted an easier way, but because he was checking out if this really was the only way. God's implicit response was that the cross was sufficient, appropriate, proportional and effective. No more punishment was needed.

There are, however, many Christians struggling with false guilt who believe this offer is for people 'better' than themselves. Very often their self-esteem has been heavily corroded over years of wrestling with the guilt-inducing accusations of their own minds. God's value of them as his precious children feels like an alien concept. They don't *feel* worthy of this offer, even though they know theoretically that unworthiness is a precondition for it. Michael Spencer wrote: 'I was a drowning man whose rescue depended on stopping all efforts to swim and trusting someone who was not going to make me a better swimmer, but who would drown in my place.'[9]

For people suffering with this level of false guilt, self-punishment can seem like the only way out. Sadly, there are few less effective methods of dealing with false guilt, primarily because it is like boxing with shadows. It is also a never-ending process, since there is no indication as to when enough punishment has taken place, or even what 'sin' the punishment is paying for. False guilt, remember, is not real; it is a mental event.

Self-punishment can take on many different forms, from the dramatic problems of self-harm and self-injury to the far more subtle variety of opportunity sabotage and pleasure withdrawal. People may choose to miss a party or another pleasant activity, or deliberately select a cheap holiday, because of their low self-worth. This is not humility or thriftiness, as it flows from self-punishment and is negative in outlook.

Many Christians use service or giving as a means of self-punishment. They may hugely overcommit to practical and sacrificial roles within the church in order to pay their 'debts'. However, these things are meant to flow from gratitude and be given freely, not be used as a means of self-justification.

Usually self-punishment is accompanied by negative 'self-talk' (the idea of the little 'devil' on your shoulder) which reaffirms a person's low value. Key self-punishment guilt narratives are:

1. You don't deserve to have this because of what you have done.
2. If people knew what you were like, they would reject you.
3. This is for good people, not for people like you.
4. Bad people do bad things; good people do good things.
5. You deserve to feel bad/feel pain; it is God punishing you.
6. Any success you have should be given back.

Self-punishment is often hidden in our churches because people feel ashamed that they are struggling to accept God's grace. The best way to begin to find freedom from this controlling issue is to come out from behind the mask and tell a 'safe' person how you actually feel. As with true guilt, acknowledging that there is a problem and understanding the problem is an important place to start.

Summary

And breathe! Having all of your most secret habits exposed in one chapter is not easy. A natural first reaction to this material may be to feel guilty, ironically, but please just sit with yourself in open acceptance. God loves you and he wants you to find freedom. Try making yourself a cup of tea and then return to the questions on the next page.

This book is not about performance, but about realism and restoration. The tools that we will explain in the next two chapters will help you to find a breakthrough.

Exercises

In chapter 3, you compared your guilty thoughts against a list of thinking styles – with which ones did you identify?

_____

_____

Here we have described the thinking style of 'jumping to conclusions'. Can you see how rumination would interact with some of the others?

_____

_____

Who do you feel you are? Impostor? Forgiven son / daughter of God? Say why you feel this.

_____

_____

Have you ever confessed the same thing several times? What did that particular 'sin' say about you?

_____

_____

Do you feel that you can receive good things from God? If not, why not?

_____

_____

Which would you say is more you? Why?
- 'I need to get everything perfect from here on.'

_____

- 'I should be punished for what I have done from here on.'

_____

6. Guilt and shame – facing feelings and actions

*It is better to risk saving a guilty person
than to condemn an innocent one.*
Voltaire, *Zadig*[1]

I (Rob) remember a particular patient who struggled with depression and false guilt. He had left an unsuccessful business which then collapsed and he mistakenly blamed himself. The fact was that it collapsed because his business partner was controlling and drank all the profits, but this was a truth he was unable to accept. He then planned a move to another part of the country to start a new life. About two weeks before moving, he changed his mind because of the sudden realization that, when he moved town, he would be taking his head with him.

Imagine you are standing on a very high bridge preparing for a bungee jump. You feel very exposed and nervous. As you move closer to the edge, more uncomfortable feelings, such as vertigo, begin to creep in. Bungee jumping is actually a huge relief, since you feel like you are getting away from these bad feelings. However, following the relief of actually doing the jump, you are wound back up to the high bridge where you begin to experience the same unpleasant feelings all over again.

When it comes to guilty emotions, many of us perpetually try to bungee jump away. We constantly distract ourselves or are incessantly busy, which brings short-term relief, but ultimately the bad feelings return. We want to encourage you to make a commitment to stay in the same uncomfortable place and face your feelings. By giving up your attempts to escape and through using the new approaches we outline, you will exchange short-term relief for long-term transformation. These next two chapters outline two groups of techniques to help you – those for guilt that is completely false or exaggerated (chapter 6), and those for guilty feelings that linger from true guilt, even after Jesus' forgiveness and personal resolution (chapter 7).

A challenge for the brave

There is a moment in C. S. Lewis's book *The Lion, The Witch and the Wardrobe* where the young Peter has to face an enemy wolf in battle. A nearby centaur could have intervened or even the lion Aslan himself, but this is a rite of passage for the future king. Only in standing firm and facing his challenger does Peter become fully aware of how to overcome him.

Mark Freeston, a professor of psychology in Newcastle, says that struggling with regular intrusive thoughts is a bit like being the local dragon slayer.[2] He says, 'It is tough to tangle with them, it is even tougher to ignore them, and even tougher still to look them squarely in the eye, issue the challenge, and then turn around and walk away (dragons really hate that!).'

The dragons of false guilt must be faced if they are to be slain; they will not be appeased and cannot be petted. The good news is that the power for victory is yours. Jesus has won the ultimate victory, and with his help you can now make the behavioural changes that will enable you to realize that victory in your day-to-day experience.

In our experience, those who wrestle with the feelings of false guilt are brave people. So often, they feel that they are unworthy, they need to repent, or that they have fallen away from God's love – when in fact they know Christ and share in the burdens that he bore. Now is the time for them to make the next step and share in his comfort. Romans 8:17 says, 'Now if we are children, then we are heirs – heirs of God and co-heirs with Christ, if indeed we share in his sufferings in order that we may also share in his glory.'

Three false-guilt slaying techniques

Here, we want to draw out three effective ways of battling with false guilt and encourage you to practise them until they become your preferred methods. They will not work every time, but using them will help you significantly to decrease the stream of falsely guilty thoughts you face. The techniques are not suppression (pushing guilty thoughts away) or avoidance (escaping through busyness, etc.). Instead, they are battles for the brave, those willing to go on the offensive.

Putting on a brave face (the extinction technique)

The dragon slayer has to look the dragon in the eye – 'because dragons really hate that' – and there is a sense that when you actually stop to examine false guilt, it diminishes in power. The difficulty is that we don't like feeling guilty, so we avoid the feeling and don't look 'the dragon' in the eye for more than a few seconds.

You may have noticed how really scary films never show you the baddy completely, or at least in normal lighting conditions. Instead, they show you shadows of them at night whilst it is also raining and windy. Your brain deals with this partial information by filling in the gaps with ideas that are far more frightening than the director can conjure up with Hollywood special effects. The extinction technique is like turning on the lights and examining your guilt dragon without any unhelpful and exaggerating mental effects.

If you take a typical falsely guilty thought, such as 'I shouldn't have felt angry in that situation', and write it down on paper, it immediately loses some of its power. At the end of chapter 1, we asked you to write down some guilty thoughts and rate each one according to how much you believed it. I expect some of you were surprised that you did not put 100% for all the lines. Now, I want you to take this further by doing a short exercise.

⇨ Take one of the thoughts from that table that you believed about 50–70% and write it at the top of a blank piece of paper.

⇨ Write it out ten times below this. How are you feeling now? How much do you believe it?

⇨ Write it out fifty times below that – use more paper! How are you feeling now? How much do you believe it?

Thought extinction exercise		
Write the thought here:		
After writing once:	*After writing ten times:*	*After writing fifty times:*
I believe the thought ____ %	I believe the thought ____ %	I believe the thought ____ %

This might seem like a boring exercise, like doing lines at school, but actually that is just the point. It might have been hard to write it out once or even a few times, as people who feel guilty can sometimes feel that they are almost making something bad happen by writing down their guilty thoughts. But the idea here is to push it to the ridiculous limit of fifty times or even more. If you are bored, you have done enough. If you are not bored, do another fifty lines. When you are bored, and nothing bad has happened and the ground has not swallowed you up, then the exercise is complete . . . The thought is extinct and robbed of its power. And well done you for being brave!

Reviewing your dragons (the appraisal technique)

In the Harry Potter books, we hear of several different types of dragon: the Hungarian Horntail, the Common Welsh Green, the Swedish Short-Snout and the Chinese Fireball.[3] To you and me, they all sound scary, but to the expert they are of differing ferocities. Guilty thoughts tend to cluster into types (what we call 'themes'). If you review your thoughts, you may find that you have three or four typical returning themes that trouble you. Examples of these could be: guilt concerning letting people down, guilt about how you feel inside, guilt about family interactions or guilt about the quality of your spiritual life, and so on. Recognizing that a thought is part of a wider theme can really help you to get it into perspective.

Returning again to your table in chapter 1 of common guilty thoughts, you will see that you can rank them according to how much you believe them. Leave the one you believe most for now – we will deal with that presently – and take the less-believed ones. Now, we are going to ask you to make an assumption – *that they are based on false guilt*. And a second assumption – *that you are overestimating how much you are actually to blame*. We hope by this stage in the book that you will have realized that these are probably safe assumptions!

Next, we want you to make a new appraisal – an alternative statement. This is not an overly positive one, but one that is based on facts and on standing back from the situation. It is the kind of advice you would give to someone else if they had your problem. Here, we want you to give the advice to yourself. Drawing on the example opposite, make new appraisals for three of your less-believed thoughts from chapter 1.

Once you have addressed individual thoughts with a new appraisal, you can take it a step further by applying a new appraisal to a whole theme and write this at the bottom of the table. This could say something like, 'I am typically bothered by letting my family down. The things I feel guilty about are exaggerated because of this sensitivity.'

We would suggest that you copy this table onto some card and keep it in your wallet. Also, stick it on the back of the toilet door and beside your bed so that you encounter it often.

	Guilty thought	Strength of belief 0–100%	New appraisal
Example:	'I shouldn't have felt angry in that situation'	60%	I cannot refuse to feel something. What I *do* with it really matters.
1			
2			
3			

The aim is to internalize the new appraisals so that you can bat away falsely guilty thoughts. In essence, you are saying, 'That is just my false guilt speaking. I have beaten that guilty thought before and I can beat it again.'

Responsibility pie (the territory technique)

People often feel guilty about things they could never have prevented, like the lady who berated herself for a burglary that followed her handbag being stolen with the keys inside. Parents feel guilty about their children's exam performances. Doctors feel guilty when one of their patients doesn't recover. Church leaders feel guilty when a congregation member falls away from fellowship.

The issue here is one of territory: are you trying to be responsible for things you neither own nor control? False guilt thrives when we believe that we are responsible for territory that is not ours. This belief has its roots in our childhood experience of the world revolving around us, when it seems that everything happens for our benefit, and conversely that we can destroy it all with one bad act. Over time, most people gain a more balanced perspective of what they are responsible for. However, if there has been trauma that interrupted development, this new perspective can be poorly formed. Some families also have an unwritten rule that everyone must be happy all of the time (and it is your responsibility to make them so).

In his book *Don't Blame Me*,[4] Tony Gough suggests there is a spectrum of responsibility. We can illustrate this using the example of a commute to work:

- things you are 100% responsible for – getting up in the morning and leaving the house
- things you are 75% responsible for – picking a fairly reliable route to work
- things you are 50% responsible for – getting on with the person sitting next to you
- things you are 25% responsible for – not being too sweaty on a hot day
- things you are not responsible for at all – the vagaries of the public transport system

If you look at your punctuality at work over a one-year period, it is mostly your responsibility to be there on time most of the time. However, consider the example of a mother who is trying to protect her toddler from germs by cleaning the house. She is plagued with thoughts that she is guilty of, and responsible for, his recent admission to hospital with a serious chest infection. Consider where children get germs from and whose 'territory' this is, as shown in the pie chart opposite.

By cleaning the house to perfection, she can still only control 20% of the dirt.

Contribution to infection

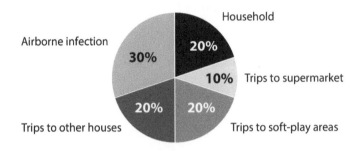

We would encourage you to sit down and complete the table and pie chart below for the thought that you believed the most in that table in chapter 1. Which parties were *also* responsible for this situation, and what percentage responsibility do they

Responsibility table	
Write the guilty thought here:	
Causes:	Percentage responsible [Total = 100%]
1:	
2:	
3:	
4:	

have? (This exercise is particularly helpful for people who have strong relational guilt themes, for example, those who blame themselves entirely for a divorce or a family division, or who feel high responsibility for the happiness of others.)

Draw your pie chart here:

How has honestly sharing responsibility affected the strength of your false guilt?

⇨ If the strength of your belief has weakened, extend your recovery with this more difficult next step. Consider what you did *not* do before because you believed the thought strongly; now *do* that thing. For example, if you have stopped driving on motorways because you believed you could be guilty of causing an accident, grab a friend and go for a drive along the piece of road you have been avoiding.

Tolerating uncertainty

We believe that these three techniques will help you significantly to reduce the impact of the majority of accusatory thoughts and feelings that extend from false guilt. Even if you are not fully convinced by them, they are usually enough to enable you to get through the day and get on with whatever you were doing. However, they will not be effective unless you can tolerate a small amount of uncertainty.

Uncertainty is not something Christians are very good at, for they have been told to be certain – especially in spiritual matters (of which false guilt can *seem* to be one). This has not been helped by two common emphases in the church, which are of course welcome but can be bad for people who need to be flexible with their false guilt. These are: (a) an anxious concern about getting the 'correct' interpretation of a passage, and (b) an emphasis on the work of the Holy Spirit to reveal all things clearly to a believer, especially 'secret sin'.

We touched on some of these things in chapter 2 and have devoted an entire chapter to it in another volume we have written called *The Worry Book*.[5] Here, all we can say is that mature and older Christians have usually discovered the secret of tolerating uncertainty (talk to some of them), and this is also a skill that can be learnt (see the exercises in our other book).

Living with future guilt threats

One of the unfortunate side effects of gaining success in reducing the frequency and intensity of false guilt is the mistaken belief that you can eradicate these sorts of thoughts for good. Ironically, this belief in itself will ensure that you will continue to suffer. You cannot live life based upon the absence of a thought, since by seeking to ensure it is *not* there, you are eternally reminding yourself of it and ensuring that it *is* there all the time. The reality is that everyone experiences appropriate true-guilt thoughts and everyone experiences inappropriate false-guilt thoughts. What makes you different is that you value the false-guilt thoughts too strongly.

For the person who struggles with false guilt, there are two ways to move forward. The first is to answer or expunge every falsely guilty thought that comes to mind. The second is to become more tolerant of these thoughts and more accepting of God's promises. Clearly, whilst we want you to be confident in dealing with individual distressing thoughts, we want this confidence to move you towards a more generalized acceptance of false guilt so that you care about it less. This may still feel 'risky', since it is still natural to worry that you might be missing true guilt, so here are a few thoughts to help you:

- We believe God is sovereign and able to deliver us from evil. (We have prayed this many times in the Lord's Prayer.)
- We believe that it is the Holy Spirit who convicts us and is able to highlight areas he wants us to grow in (and that we don't need to become obsessed with 'the search' ourselves).
- We believe that experimenting with our responses to false guilt is essential to making the changes that will lead to greater freedom.

What is clear is that, without any experiments, we will never really know if change really is possible, as this analogy illustrates.

Rory got on the London train and sat down opposite a small man in a suit. As they left the station, the small man began tearing his newspaper into tiny pieces and throwing it out of the window. Rory pretended it wasn't happening, but after a while felt compelled to ask, 'What on earth are you doing?' The small man replied, 'It's very simple. I am keeping elephants off the track.' 'But there aren't any elephants on the track!' exclaimed Rory. The small man smiled and said, 'It must be working then . . .'

This rather daft story illustrates two points of view. To the small man, the act of throwing paper onto the track kept the elephants away and made the train safe. To Rory, the train was already safe because there were no elephants anywhere near the track – because this was the south of England after all! But who was right? The only way to find out was to stop throwing the paper out of the window – something the small man had never done because his protective belief and subsequent action were self-reinforcing.[6]

Here are two experiments you may wish to have a go at.[7] There are many that can be done, but we have selected these two as the most helpful to start with. Please do consider other experiments, but try to tackle the less scary things first, until you have built up your confidence.

1. Being out of control
David tried to keep a tight control on his thoughts. He was worried that he might think an evil or a blasphemous thought. He was worried that if he did, his thoughts would spiral out of control and he would go mad or go to hell. He was able to see that there was an alternative possibility – that his thoughts would not spiral and that he would stay sane and not think anything that bad. He decided to compare extra-strict thought control with no control at all. He planned a day of each and prepared for the experiment by reflecting on the fact that he had not gone mad yet.

On the 'strict-control' day, he reported that he struggled even more than usual, with high levels of anxiety and guilt. On the other day, he merely noted the thoughts and wrote them down instead of suppressing them – this gave him the slight pause he needed. He actually felt *more* in control! He did not go mad or feel particularly guilty.

2. Being an imperfectionist

Jane tried to always do things perfectly. This included dressing well, believing this would make others less likely to think badly of her. If she was less than perfectly presented, she felt guilty and anticipated being excluded by the group. However, she was able to see an alternative perspective that others would not actually mind or even notice. To prepare, she kept a diary of what others wore and to her surprise noticed that work colleagues sometimes wore clothes for two days running with small stains – she had never noticed this before, and it made her less anxious in trying her experiment.

On the chosen day, she put a small amount of gravy on her top and went to work. She was anxious, but it was bearable and she could still work. Nobody noticed the stain, so the next day she made it bigger. Still nobody noticed, and even when she said, 'Oh, silly me, I have spilt my breakfast on me . . .', nobody seemed to care. Over time, she was able to challenge other behaviours, such as always having to be super-early for deadlines. And her falsely guilty feelings began to weaken.

Building the confidence to stop reacting

As we mentioned earlier in this section, our ultimate aim is that you can find greater freedom from false guilt and greater acceptance of your uncertainty that it really is 'false'. The difficulty in treating these sorts of thoughts in Christians is their desire always to be on the safe side. Unfortunately, the typical compulsion to act against their thoughts or feelings serves only to strengthen their false beliefs.

Martin Luther (1483–1546), the great Protestant Reformer, felt so guilty and haunted by impure thoughts that he even saw visions of the devil – on one occasion throwing his ink pot at him. He had real trouble in allowing these thoughts to go unchecked. Yet, over time, he was able to apply more of the doctrine of grace to himself.

We pray that, through increasing your understanding and your confidence in identifying false guilt over true guilt, you will learn to react less, not more. This has two benefits: firstly, you experience greater freedom; secondly, the strength and frequency of the thoughts and feelings reduce. In the end, there are two possible realities here – either something *is* very important or something *seems* very important. But which is true?

> Fiona was troubled with intrusive and unwelcome sexual thoughts about sleeping with the man across the road. She believed this meant she was somehow deeply bad and sinful, and even her Christian faith was not enough to transform her. She tried to be a good Christian and repress these thoughts, but this seemed to make them bubble up all the more.
>
> Each time one of these thoughts entered her head, she felt terribly guilty and she had to pray to Jesus to save her from what she had done and take away her guilt. She then got relief for a while, until the next guilty thought came. They came several times a day, and it took several prayers to shift each one. She was trapped in a vicious

circle. Over time, her prayer had become more complex, so she now had to pray for about four things and use some Bible verses to feel better.

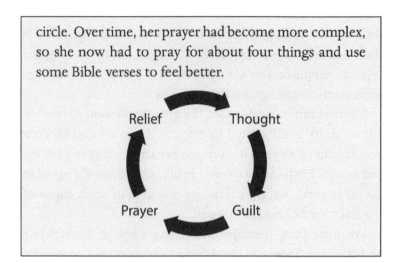

Relief — Thought — Guilt — Prayer

If Fiona was to set up an experiment to see whether she was dealing with true or false guilt, it might look something like the one below. She knew that doing any kind of experiment was likely to make things a bit more stressful at the start, so she focused on the medium- and long-term outcomes.

Stage 1 – Predicting

She predicted what would happen if she stopped praying to Jesus each time she got a guilty thought, considering what would happen if (as she feared) she was truly guilty, or (as she hoped) that this was a psychological problem called false guilt. She checked out her logic with a trusted friend.

- If she was truly guilty, she predicted that the Holy Spirit would increase his attempts to convict her of her sin and that her sinful nature would generate many more of the thoughts now it had been given half a chance.
- If this was all false guilt, then she would no longer be driving the vicious circle and over time she would have

fewer guilty thoughts. However, she predicted that they might initially be worse, as she would not be using her usual safety behaviours. Her true nature as a child of God would be able to flourish, rather than being preoccupied with thought suppression.

She then considered the risks.

- If she carried on as previously, she would probably be wracked with guilt all her life. She might have achieved holiness in one small area by repenting of these thoughts, but her worship and witness would be very restricted.
- If the experiment showed it to be false guilt, then she would be more free and able to live a full Christian life, more able to be committed in her worship and securely on the path to heaven in the arms of God's grace. There was a small chance the experiment would mislead her – but just a small one.

On balance, she decided to go for it – in stages, starting with something easy first.

Stage 2 – Experimenting

She picked a time and place where she wouldn't be disturbed for about an hour and brought one of her intrusive thoughts to mind. She started with something towards the less-sinful-sounding end of what she struggled with – thinking about holding the man's hand.

She measured these things with a simple rating scale from $0 \to 10$, making a note of her score every five minutes. If she was really struggling not to pray for relief, she would stand up and focus out of the window for a few minutes of respite.

She was aware that Satan (genuinely this time!) would not want her to be doing this experiment to be free from his false guilt, so she had asked a friend to pray for her whilst she was doing this work.

Stage 3 – Reviewing

As expected, things were quite tough for about half an hour, and then she became more relaxed and she still had not prayed. After an hour and a half, she felt a mixture of boredom and exhaustion but was no longer anxious. There was still a nagging guilt, but much less intense now.

Repeating this every day for a week removed most of the rest of the guilt, and she was able to enjoy her faith much more than before. She was also a lot less stressed and depressed.

The experiment had proved it was false guilt. This was not about her relaxing her standards; it was about her realizing that the way she was thinking was holding her captive. If anything, she was now a flourishing Christian and really able to engage with worship without distraction.

Summary

This chapter has helped you to address false guilt in two ways: firstly, we helped you to apply three direct (dragon-slaying) techniques to false guilt: extinction, appraisal and territory techniques. Secondly, we introduced the idea that becoming tolerant of the thoughts and feelings surrounding false guilt can give you the edge for long-term recovery.

We have also explained how the particular anxieties of Christian believers regarding 'being on the safe side' can be detrimental to recovery and actually keep the false-guilt cycle alive. We would strongly advise you to go back over this chapter several times to ensure that you understand the experiments. It is then essential to actually have a go at them yourself. Remember that some initial discomfort is totally normal, and more than this, it actually shows that you are doing the experiment correctly.

Exercises

What did you take away from the dragon-slayer analogy? Is there anything that does not make sense?

_____

_____

_____

Which of the three dragon-slaying techniques made most sense to you? Why?
- The extinction technique
- The appraisal technique
- The territory technique

_____

_____

_____

Make some notes here about when you tried one of these techniques:

The _____ technique

_____

_____

_____

_____

Do you try to control your thoughts? Did you try David's experiment?

_____

_____

Are you a perfectionist? Did you try Jane's experiment?

_____

_____

Are there times when you are worried about whether your guilt is actually affecting your salvation? If so, try the 'ultimate experiment' and make your plans here:

- Predicting

  _____

  _____

  _____

- Experimenting

  _____

  _____

  _____

- Reviewing

  _____

  _____

  _____

7. Accepting forgiveness – living in the present

The courage to be is the courage to accept oneself,
in spite of being unacceptable.
Paul Tillich, *The Courage to Be*[1]

Nicola was driving home late at night after a stressful day at the office. It was raining and dark, but she wasn't really focused on the road. A text message from her anxious husband buzzed on the seat next to her, and she glanced down at the bright screen. In the next few seconds, Nicola lost control and ploughed into the back of a car that was waiting at the red traffic lights ahead.

Eight years later, Nicola thinks about that accident every day. She remembers the child who was seriously injured because of her careless driving. She reminds herself that she has a criminal record and she tells herself that she doesn't deserve anything good in life. This is despite knowing the full forgiveness of Jesus and having received a letter from the child's parents offering her forgiveness.

In the last chapter, we gave you some very clear techniques to use to address false guilt and showed examples of people who had intrusive and unwelcome thoughts that caused them distress. You may have got to this point in the book and have been asking, 'But what if I really did do something wrong, something for which I rightly felt true guilt but something I just can't get over?'

Here, we want to help you to deal with the experience of true guilt that has been truly forgiven by God and yet has not been forgiven by you.

Guilt getting personal

There is a similar word to 'guilt', and that is 'shame'. The two terms are used somewhat interchangeably, as we touched on in the first chapter, but they actually have distinct meanings. Guilt is the feeling that I have done something wrong and owe something (it has its roots in the German word *Geld*, meaning money or debt); shame, on the other hand, relates to our sense of who we are and our need to conceal or hide an aspect of ourselves.[2] As such, it clings more closely to our identity, as it is not about our actions but about our very self. We feel ashamed, embarrassed, ostracized and cast out.

Professor Paul Gilbert helpfully emphasizes that guilt and shame are not dissociated emotions, but easy bedfellows. 'Guilt can trigger shame, and self-attacking thoughts, such as "I am a cheat and a bad/unlovable person."'[3] If you wonder what keeps your wrestling with guilt so much alive, it is not the fear of your mistakes so much as what you believe they say about you.

We can also respond aggressively when challenged – due to low self-esteem, we can 'act out' rather than be found out. Heinz Kohut, a psychoanalyst, described shame as a 'narcissistic wound'[4] – you might think narcissism is a good thing to wound, but remember how dangerous a wounded animal can be. They will do anything rather than admit their weakness.

Why is the reaction so extreme? It is because we fear
something far deeper than nagging guilt. Paul Tournier says,
'In every age, men . . . picture God as one who loves them
only on condition that they are good, and who refuses to love
them if they become guilty. Fear of losing the love of God –
this is the essence of our human problem and of psychology.'[5]
Simply put: our guilt for the things we have done tips into
shame for who we believe we are, which subsequently morphs
into anxiety that we will be totally rejected and abandoned.

This combination of sadness and desperation and rejection
can be seen in the story of Jean Valjean in Victor Hugo's
Les Misérables.

> Jean Valjean knows something of both guilt and shame.
> He has served his term in prison and just been paroled
> to live as a beggar, made to carry the 'yellow ticket' of
> an ex-con. He spends a night in a bishop's house but,
> instead of just accepting their food, he steals the silver.
> Police bring him back to face the bishop who, instead of
> asking for charges to be pressed, gives him yet more
> silver and tells him how much God loves him.
>
> In the musical of *Les Misérables*, Jean Valjean sings a
> song: 'What Have I Done?' The bishop could have cast
> him out, but instead he invites him to walk with God.
> Valjean is amazed that the bishop seems to know what
> is going on inside him (all the shame and guilt) and yet
> still tells him he has a soul and is loved by God. He does
> not understand.
>
> Valjean goes on in the story to show how a man can
> 'get' grace and rebuild his life. He had more than paid
> for his original crime – stealing a loaf of bread. He knows
> he has paid for his *guilt*. Instead, what he struggled with

more was his *shame* – the idea that he might not be able to love himself again.

He makes a fair start, growing a business and living as an honest man – eventually becoming the city's mayor. But even this is hollow and based on a false identity. It is only later in the film that he comes clean and overcomes his shame. Here he sings a song called: 'Who Am I?', which gets (literally) to the heart of the matter.

This is contrasted with his adversary, the policeman Javert, who does not understand grace and instead lives by his works and a set of absolute rules, repressing his guilt. Javert ultimately takes his own life, ashamed by Valjean's kindness, as his internal world becomes more and more conflicted – being challenged by love.[6]

One of the great things about the Christian community is that it is made up of people who are significantly less than perfect. They may still question and doubt but, like Valjean, they aim for something more beautiful. Sadly, some churches do not give this impression – people's guilt and shame are actually exploited. However, Christianity at its best welcomes and loves all. It has been described as 'one bunch of beggars telling another bunch of beggars where to find bread'.[7]

To call someone a beggar or 'untouchable' is to make an identity statement – unwashed, unnamed, unloved. Then, let us be beggars together in this! Only then can God reach out and call to us – washed, named, loved. Only when our guilt and shame are on the table can we truly know how great his love and mercy are, and how we have moved from being outcasts to being adopted sons and daughters.

To have a mature faith is to know that, despite your doubts and shortcomings, God still loves you. Brennan Manning,

Franciscan priest and author, said, 'To live by grace means to acknowledge my whole life story, the light side and the dark. In admitting my shadow side, I learn who I am and what God's grace means.'[8]

The quote by philosopher Paul Tillich at the start of this chapter is similar, asking us to realize at a deep level that we will never be perfect this side of heaven. The Bible is full of similar statements. Jesus said, 'It is not the healthy who need a doctor, but those who are ill. I have not come to call the righteous, but sinners' (Mark 2:17). He even said, 'Blessed are those who hunger and thirst for righteousness' (Matthew 5:6).

If you still hunger for peace and thirst for freedom from guilt, know that you are truly blessed, for these are godly aims and 'be-attitudes'! Deep grace is a state of mind where we *know* we are forgiven, *even though* we do not feel it, and where we live out our faith all the more because we know how sweet this is.

Matt Redman writes in his song 'You Alone Can Rescue':

Who, oh Lord, could save themselves,
Their own soul could heal?
Our shame was deeper than the sea.
Your grace is deeper still.[9]

Giving up your grievance story

Guilt can be paralysing! As we saw in the life of Nicola at the beginning of this chapter, many people relive their guilt every day, despite knowing the real forgiveness of God. In his book, *Forgive for Good*,[10] Dr Fred Luskin describes our typical development of a 'grievance story': 'When we are talking about grievances and wounds, the way we create our story will be of the utmost importance.'[11]

People who struggle to let go of their forgiven guilt are actually struggling with a grievance story that they have built up against themselves. Very often these stories are fuelled by the shame we described earlier and reaffirm their intrinsic 'badness'. Equally, these stories tend to make unreachable demands like: 'Only if this event hadn't really happened, can I move on with my life.' People can become consumed by arguing against the grievance narrative that they themselves have constructed.

To get the best out of the tools we will illustrate in this chapter, you must decide that now is the moment to give up your grievance story. Luskin says,

> Understanding that holding grudges and creating a grievance story are not the best approaches to letting go of anger and frustration is in essence a type of self forgiveness . . . Self forgiveness is both a beneficial part of the forgiveness process and a necessary skill in learning to overcome being upset with ourselves.[12]

Remember that only God can forgive true guilt, but self-forgiveness is about internalizing the truth of his forgiveness. This is an act of humility, as we agree that his-story, not our story, is victorious.

Take a moment prayerfully to hand over your grievance story to God.

Learning self-compassion

If you are British like me, you probably suffer from what is both a national strength and a failing – the inability to speak well of yourself. We are modest and self-effacing to a fault.

Being humble is of course a wonderful thing to aim for and mentioned many times in the Bible. But being humble is not the same as being a doormat and allowing others to walk over you. The person who struggles with guilt usually does a fair job of walking all over themselves. This can be a problem when our starting point in dealing with others is how we deal with 'me'. In fact, we can be significantly better and more loving to others than we ever are to ourselves. As Dr John Lockley states,

> The Bible says that we are to love our neighbours as ourselves – but to many a guilt-ridden Christian the problem is far more cogently stated as, 'learn to treat yourself as you would your neighbour'. This is not easily done . . .[13]

The answer to this is surprisingly simple. God calls us to love our neighbour, on the basis of choice, not sentiment. You can be kind to someone you do not like. You can be generous and

It is OK to be cruel to myself because . . .	Is this present? ☑
I have messed things up and deserve to feel like this	
It keeps me on my toes, so I don't miss anything I need to do something about	
Other people are nasty to me (or look down on me) so they must be right	
It prepares me in advance for when others are cruel to me	
Your reason	
Your reason	

understanding. It might not be the whole story and is some way short of love just now, but it can be a place to start. So, can you be kind to yourself as an act of choice today?

The first step to being kind is to stop being cruel. There are many reasons why people justify cruelty to themselves. Which of these in the table on the previous page do you identify with?

As you will see from the list, many people who struggle with guilt have an overdeveloped ability to self-criticize – and conversely an underdeveloped ability to self-soothe.

Self-soothing

Developing the ability to self-soothe is the key way to move from being someone who struggles with guilt to someone who is able to let it wash over them and soothe themselves as this happens.

We all have spikes of guilt, but what marks out the person who struggles with problem guilt is that the spikes stick around and they then have a jolly good go at themselves.

Self-soothing is a skill and it will take some practice. Below are the basic principles and some exercises to try. These might sound trite and simplistic, and some of them have been ridiculed by Hollywood films, but give them a go in private and see what happens.

- Recall a 'safe place', which could be a past positive memory, and spend some time thinking about it. Describe it to yourself in some detail, so that you can 'go there' when times are tough. You might like to paint a picture of it or get a photo from the internet and keep it in your wallet/purse.[14]

- Practise a 'half-smile', one with contentment and no tension. If it helps, use an icon to meditate on – maybe a picture of Jesus with this kind of smile. Start with his smile and then transfer this to your smile.
- Some people take this one step further and practise laughing out loud – even if you do not feel like laughing. Laughing at yourself is a good way to train mental strength. It also stimulates endorphins. It is forced, yes, but it is a start.
- Try 'compassionate re-evaluating' – this is generating a feeling of warmth (perhaps by using a half-smile), then rereading the 'reasons to be cruel' you listed in the table on page 142 and choosing instead to be kind to yourself. What do you notice? Do you believe them as strongly now?

These techniques are hard to master, and it is beyond the scope of this book to teach them fully. If this suggestion resonates with you, we would recommend that you find a good therapist and let them help you practise.[15]

Another tip is momentarily to agree to suspend your critical thinking – it's OK, you can come back to it later! This will help you take a break from the stream of critical thoughts to try out some kind ones. You may even find you do not want/need to come back . . . Remember that these are most likely on account of false guilt and that you have already repented of all your true guilt. Consider how much more able you would be to grow in your faith if you could feel a bit better for a while. Now practise one of the techniques above.

ACT compassionately towards yourself
Our brains are tricky things, and sometimes it is easier just to do something and hope your emotions and thoughts follow.

Actually, they often do – especially if you can do the right thing for you. Which of the things in the list below would you find most tricky to do – perhaps because you do not feel you deserve it? Start with one of the easier things and work up towards the one you struggle most to do.

Things I can do to be kind to myself are . . .	Rank these in order of difficulty 1 to 6
Pray with your eyes open and hands facing up – this is a posture of being accepted and expecting to receive. Can you do this before God?	
Give yourself a small gift – maybe a trip to the cinema or something nice for the bath/shower. Can you treat yourself for no other reason than that it is a treat?	
Take up a friend on one of their offers to help you out. Maybe they have offered to babysit or do some ironing or give you a lift. Don't offer to repay them – that can come later. Can you accept help and offer nothing back in return?	
Dress up in some nice clothes and put on some make-up. Go for a short walk – no-one is asking for any more. Can you make yourself look beautiful?	
Your idea	
Your idea	

THINK compassionately towards yourself

The exercises and suggestions in the last two sections have emphasized the benefits of receiving the compassion of others (therapists) and the self (self-soothing). Now, we want to examine our hurtful thinking. People who struggle with false guilt often have a very low and critical estimation of themselves. They use very black-and-white thinking processes that typically leave them coming up short and feeling unrealistically guilty and negative about themselves.

We have gently introduced 'compassion' as something that can be materially *felt* through interactions with others or *experienced* through self-directed exercises like those on the list above. However, the greatest benefits of compassion will be felt when they are integrated into your actual *mindset*. By this, we mean moving beyond just appreciating why compassion is important to actually embedding it in your day-to-day thought pattern.

We hope that having experienced the benefits of compassion from others and self-soothing, you will become more able to accept them from yourself. Before we go further, here are five common reasons why people refuse to nurture a more compassionate mindset. Which of these do you recognize?

1. I don't believe I deserve to be compassionate to myself.
2. The things I am saying to myself seem untrue.
3. It feels a bit sickly to talk to myself kindly. I'm not that sort of person.
4. I am worried I will let myself off the hook for real sin.
5. I can't see the point in trying to be compassionate to myself.

Starting a compassionate mindset

Firstly, to challenge number 5 above, recall the compassion of others you have experienced. We do not want your thinking to become unreal or based on imagination, but simply much more like the 'mind of Christ' which is all compassion to you. Working in the spirit of Romans 12:2 ('Be transformed by the renewing of your mind . . .'), developing a compassionate mindset begins with accepting that your current thinking is not perfectly true or good and offering yourself more compassionate alternative thoughts. You can look at the other objections in similar ways.

Of course, introducing new thoughts will feel strange at first, and initially more unbelievable, yet over time your mind will strengthen them, and they will take the place of less realistic negative outlooks. Importantly, the compassion you offer yourself will help you to be more realistic about your false guilt and far better placed to win the battles that we discussed in the preceding chapter. Beginning to use a compassionate mindset is simply to imagine you are talking warmly of your dearest friends, listening to them and offering them compassionate understanding. Not pearls of wisdom, chipped in from a distance, but heartfelt interactions among those who journey together.

This is not being soft on yourself – in fact, it is an incredibly hard thing to do. Professor Paul Gilbert, in his book *The Compassionate Mind*, says, 'Self-warmth may develop from genuine sympathy for your own distress and gentleness towards your needs. It's not however to be confused with self-centredness or feeling that you are following your own agenda. It arises from enabling yourself to feel compassion from the inside.'[16] Increasing your ability to console, nurture and sympathize with yourself directly challenges the harsh and ungodly voice that so many of us use for self-attacking.

Growing in self-nurture not only connects deeply with God's love for you as his forgiven child, but also increases your ability to offer his compassion to God's other children.

Compassionate narrative exercise

Use the following Bible verses as prompts for your new compassionate narrative. Allow your self-esteem and self-warmth to grow as the truth of God becomes the truth you treat yourself with.

- John 1:12 — I am God's child.
- 1 Corinthians 6:19–20 — I have been bought with a price and I belong to God.
- 1 Corinthians 12:27 — I am a member of Christ's body.
- Ephesians 1:3–8 — I have been chosen by God and adopted as his child.
- Colossians 1:13–14 — I have been redeemed and forgiven of all my sins.
- Romans 8:31–39 — I am free from any condemnation brought against me and I cannot be separated from the love of God.
- Colossians 3:1–4 — I am hidden with Christ in God.
- Philippians 1:6 — I am confident that God will complete the good work he started in me.
- 1 John 5:18 — I am born of God and the evil one cannot touch me.
- John 15:5 — I am a branch of Jesus Christ, the true vine, and a channel of his life.
- John 15:16 — I have been chosen and appointed to bear fruit.
- 1 Corinthians 3:16 — I am God's temple.

Getting help to get over guilt

Recovering from the type of guilt we have been describing in this chapter can be a long journey, but it is very attainable. Sometimes, working with a compassionate professional is the best way to move forward, not least because you will actually experience compassion and acceptance from an objective source. This takes time – time to develop trust and the space in which to do it. Therapists call this the 'therapeutic space' and they do not just mean the room in which they see their clients. To be sure, the room is important, which is why if you look up 'therapist' on the internet, you will usually see quiet and pastel-shaded rooms with the ever-present box of tissues.

The 'therapeutic hour' is another important term – not always an exact hour, but always a pre-arranged length of time when the therapist will do their utmost to be there for you. Being there is not just literal (though a good therapist will always arrive early and give ample notice of upcoming holidays), it is also emotional (putting their own issues to one side for a while to listen to you). For this reason, the therapist needs their own therapy, for some of their patients may be very difficult or even annoying, but their role here is to love.

Questions are allowed

In this therapeutic space, all kinds of questions can be asked. They start with simple questions of trust like: 'will this therapist be here for me next week?' or 'what will happen if I turn up late?' Hence, the journey starts with simply accepting the client where they are – overzealous attempts to change someone right from the start of therapy can actually make him or her feel unaccepted. After all, God accepts us just as we are.

The questions can then move on to ones about love. The therapist 'holds' the client's fears about being unlovable and so shows them they are not as bad as they feared. Paul Tournier likens this to Jesus addressing the woman caught in adultery in John chapter 8: '[Jesus] does not suggest that she has not sinned, but he refuses to pronounce any condemnation.'[17]

By 'holding' the client's guilt and shame for a while, the therapist allows it to come into the conscious for long enough to be examined for what it is. If it is newly realized true guilt, it can be prayerfully addressed; if it is false guilt, appropriate tools can be employed; and if it is lingering guilt from a lack of self-forgiveness, this too can be dealt with. The key encouragement we want to leave with you is that you are a precious child of God, he has compassion on you and he longs for you to know the riches of his grace to the depths of your heart. If counselling is needed to help get there, then so be it.

Summary

We have looked at the importance of a deep, or rich, understanding of grace as a journey. There will be ups and downs along the way, but God loves and forgives us all the same.

We looked at the power of grievance stories in blocking our experience of true forgiveness, and you have seen some techniques for starting to be, and act, more compassionately towards yourself. We looked at how growing a compassion- ate mindset offers us a rich and more godly alternative to self-attacking thinking styles, and in turn how much more this sort of thinking resonates with God's own approach to us. Lastly, we have seen how the 'therapeutic space' can start with acceptance, and then build trust and enable questions to be asked about love.

Exercises

Can you relate to Nicola's story at the start of the chapter? Which life events are you clinging on to?

_____

_____

_____

What is your grievance story against yourself? Write it here.

_____

_____

_____

How good are you at getting guilt / shame into your conscious awareness to examine it – or do you tend to repress it the moment it surfaces?

_____

_____

_____

Which of the 'self-soothing' ideas did you try? What did you learn?

_____

_____

_____

Which of the 'compassionate-act' tasks did you try? Were any of them too hard to do just now?

_____

_____

_____

How is your compassionate mind growing and how has your inner narrative changed?

_____

_____

_____

Which of the Bible verses in the final section did you find most helpful in offering yourself self-warmth?

_____

_____

_____

Have you ever seen a counsellor or therapist? Would it be helpful for you to see one? (See details in Appendix 2, p. 180.) What was your experience of the 'therapeutic space'?

_____

_____

_____

8. Guilt and joy – a better journey

Fear will hold you captive; hope will set you free.
Red, in *The Shawshank Redemption*

Turning the inside out

At the very beginning of this book, we introduced you to a prisoner who had been released and yet remained in his cell, unable to take the few short steps through the open door. Over the first seven chapters, Rob and I have tried to address those things, both internal and external, that bound him to false guilt and kept him from embracing the forgiven life we have in Jesus Christ.

As someone who struggles with guilt and can understand the prisoner's position, how do you feel now? How many steps have you taken towards the door? What do you need to do to go further? What do you think might be holding you back?

⇨ *Notes:*

_____

_____

_____

People who struggle with false guilt have inverted the typical human approach to self-preservation: instead of being critical of others and unforgiving, they will struggle to have a bad opinion of anyone, and will forgive others for anything, but not themselves. Their aggression is pointed inwards, and their compassion is pointed outwards. They also weave distortions of Christian theology around niceness, passivity and humility, and the prison is no longer four walls and barred windows – but the heart.

We have taken some steps to shift the polarities of hostility and compassion. In chapter 6, we emphasized the need to direct your hostility outwards towards the 'guilt dragons', encouraging you to use three active techniques (extinction, appraisal and territory) to fight back. These were balanced by a new approach to self-nurture and self-compassion in chapter 7, which welcomes the true forgiveness and love we receive in Jesus Christ. Now, it is time to take this even further. It's time to assert your rights and turn your inner aggression to outer assertiveness.

My 'bill of rights'

False guilt smothers your sense of entitlement to anything good. It makes us passive and tries to cow us into quiet submission. David Seamands wrote,

> Satan's greatest psychological weapon is a gut feeling of inferiority, inadequacy and low self-worth. This feeling shackles many Christians, in spite of wonderful spiritual experiences and knowledge of God's word. Although they understand their position as sons and daughters of God, they are tied up in knots, bound by a terrible feeling of inferiority, and chained to a deep sense of worthlessness.[1]

My bill of rights	Rank these in order of importance to you
I have the right to enjoy the complete forgiveness that Jesus offers me.	
I have the right to inherent worth, not dictated by what I have or have not done, but coming directly from God.	
I have the right to receive forgiveness without shame when I make new mistakes.	
I have the right to accept the mistakes of my past without punishing myself for them today.	
I have the right to express myself, my needs and my desires, despite my feelings of guilt.	
I have the right to enjoy and engage fully in my activities without them being hijacked by the agenda of guilt.	
I have the right to be assertive and angry when that is appropriate and necessary.	
Your rights ideas . . .	

The Bible says that you have authority. When explaining to the first disciples about the authority they had, Jesus said, 'I have given you authority to trample on snakes and scorpions and to overcome all the power of the enemy; nothing will harm you' (Luke 10:19). It is time to take the authority of a child of God and turn your hostility away from yourself and against false guilt. Take up your 'bill of rights'.

Please note, we are not asking you to become aggressive and domineering – that would be going too far. Too often today, people focus on rights and pay no attention to responsibility. However, we are suggesting that you start to regain a balance in your world – where there has probably been too little 'right' and too much responsibility.

What is keeping me from my 'rights'

We hope you feel stirred up when you read out your rights and that you have added some of your own to the list. You may want to draw out the table and stick it alongside your mirror, so that each day you can begin on the offensive with false or lingering guilt. However, as you will know by now, freedom does not come easily to us in this area, and there are a few more things to remind you of if the 'bill of rights' is going to be more than just a nice sentiment.

My (Will's) daughter has a little rabbit which we call 'Rabbitiroo'. This small flannel toy is the key to successful sleep and general comfort. To lose Rabbitiroo is a catastrophe of biblical proportions, and therefore extreme care is constantly employed to ensure that we know its whereabouts at all times. The strange thing about this precious toy is that no other child is jealous to possess it, and most adults keep their distance from it as if it were some kind of biohazard (which it possibly is).

Many of us carry our own false guilt around with us like Rabbitiroo. No-one is jealous of us for possessing it; it is a hazard to our well-being and yet we grip it so tightly that there is little hope that we will ever drop it on the supermarket floor. Whereas our conscience was once a bright and helpful thing, it has now become frayed and distorted, bringing with it not joy and transformation, but despair and self-loathing. However, it is very familiar to us. We may have been carrying it for decades, and therefore, despite knowing it is toxic, both habit and familiarity are keeping us together.

Attached to guilt

It would be easy to become irritated, especially by my suggestion that you are somehow attached to false guilt when you are doing everything in your power to get rid of it. But the best way to understand this important idea is to look at other unhappy life attachments like smoking, alcohol or drugs. I have met hundreds of addicts over the years, and not a single one has defended their attachment to a substance, and yet every one of them has struggled to break it. Behind the attachments are either beliefs or threats that are somehow mitigated by the *presenting* addiction.

The list of 'I' statements opposite refers to many of the key points already made within this book and offers a clearer indication of which beliefs make false guilt hard to let go of. Write your responses to these 'I' statements, based on what you have read in this book – think of this as being akin to a revision exercise.

There will be other factors outside of your influence which mean that you cannot move fully away from guilt. We looked at these in chapter 4, and they include your natural 'proneness' to guilt, any mental illness, your family situation and the

My 'I' statement	My response
I deserve punishment . . .	
I feel bad, so I must have done something wrong . . .	
I need to be certain . . .	
I need to be safe . . .	
I am always to blame . . .	
I don't deserve success . . .	
Your own 'I' statement	

(We have put the 'answers' at the end of this chapter)

accusations of others. If these are still very prevalent, we would encourage you to pay special attention to the next sections on having kindness and compassion towards yourself.

True self-compassion rooted in Jesus

Loving yourself just because we tell you to or because a cosmetics company says, 'You're worth it!' is just empty love. It is like telling all children that they are good at sport when it is self-evident that this is not the case. Instead, it is much more helpful to make accurate and specific comments about a person's abilities and lack of abilities – 'I am not good at football, but I am good at music.' This is where confidence is to be found, not in the hollow positive-self talk of the self-esteem movement.[2]

Jesus gives us two starting points for our self-compassion – that we are guilty, but that he loves us nonetheless. And this is not a theoretical love, but a deeply compassionate love. However, remember the fig leaf. We cannot accept this love until we abandon other attempts to fix the problem or boost our self-esteem. In this back-to-front section, we look at how, in order to win the battle against guilt, you first have to lose it.

Abandoning abandonment

True guilt is a helpful emotion that directs us away from negative behaviours into positive ones. It leads to growth, relational harmony and societal cohesion. Most importantly, it makes us aware of our deep need for Jesus Christ and the grace that he offers us through his death and resurrection. At the same time, those of us who struggle with false guilt have found that, despite the good news of the Christian message, we have been unable to let go of our guilt and fully give up the search for whatever we believe excludes us.

Terry D. Cooper says, 'Even when we deeply value ourselves, the anxiety ... will tempt us to find our source of security in some strategy rather than a trust in God.'[3] Many of us are so bound by the fear of deserving abandonment because of our guilt and shame, we cannot let go of the very things we are desperate to let go of. Malcolm France says, in the aptly named *The Paradox of Guilt*, 'Fear is the enemy that keeps us from the place of healing. For the great majority of us, fear will prevent us accepting total loss until such a time as fear itself is overruled by death.'[4]

The 'total loss' France is referring to is the greatest and most unique weapon available to Christians who are afflicted by false guilt. Accepting 'total loss' is to abandon totally our natural defences against abandonment, completely disempowering and defusing the cycle of false guilt in our lives. It's time to give up in order to get up.

Killing the impostor spirit

False guilt and the subsequent shame lead us to develop an 'impostor spirit'.[5] The impostor seeks to blend in, but ultimately feels as if he or she will be 'found out' at any moment. The impostor becomes brilliant at repressing or diverting their true feelings and desires. Fuelled by the anxiety that we are not good enough, it both works tirelessly to 'look' good and constantly seeks out reasons why we should be abandoned. Conflict is avoided at all costs.

St Paul was a murderer of Christians and a persecutor of the church before his miraculous conversion, and you could say he had much to feel guilty about.[6] His ministry was at times impacted by his experience of being in conflict with the early apostles, most clearly expressed in Acts 15:2, yet Paul would not be cowed by an 'impostor spirit'; he would not become deferential to the other apostles because they 'deserved' their authority more (see also Galatians 2).

What enabled St Paul to live so freely and confidently? Well, it wasn't his credentials or achievements. Paul could well have allowed the 'impostor spirit' to become his defence against abandonment and the justification for his position. In Philippians 3:4–6 he says,

> If others think they have reasons to put confidence in the flesh, I have more: circumcised on the eighth day, of the people of Israel, of the tribe of Benjamin, a Hebrew of Hebrews; in regard to the law, a Pharisee; as for zeal, persecuting the church; as for righteousness based on the law, faultless.

Instead of allowing the 'impostor spirit' to rob him of his freedom and make him a slave to false guilt and fear, Paul does the reverse. He kills the 'impostor spirit' by embracing his total lack of qualification for anything good. In verse 8, he says, 'I consider everything a loss because of the surpassing worth of knowing Christ Jesus my Lord, for whose sake I have lost all things.' When it comes to guilt, instead of trying to grade his sins to see if he is as bad as he may fear, he simply argues that he should be accepted completely, because the whole reason why Christ Jesus came into the world was to save sinners just like him.

Total loss is total gain

If false guilt is kept alive by our fear of abandonment, then by 'accepting completely' that we are the 'worst sinner of all', we defuse the worst of what we fear. Accepting total loss means the game is up and we can stop fighting. The great news is that whether or not we have been wrestling with false guilt or true, God's love for us is complete and eternal. He cannot abandon himself and, as he dwells within us, we shall never be abandoned. Thomas Merton says, 'Surrender your poverty and acknowledge your nothingness to the Lord. Whether you understand it or not, God loves you, lives in you, dwells in you, calls you, saves you and offers you an understanding and compassion which are like nothing you have ever found in a book or heard in a sermon.'[7]

Our level of trust in something often seems related to our circumstances: a difficult decision, a tough job, an illness or a period of uncertainty. Yet, I believe that the greatest trust we can exhibit within the Christian life is simply to surrender to Christ. Life's greatest irony is surely that abandonment to Christ causes the greatest restoration of our identity. Being abandoned to Christ is actually being found by God.

Look back over the last section. Give your first response to the following statements:	Your response
I am attached to my guilt because . . .	
My 'impostor spirit' is expressed in . . .	
The word 'abandonment' makes me think . . .	
Trusting Jesus for my reputation, relationships and future feels . . .	

A gentle journey of surrender

Seeing your first responses to these statements written down might be something of a shock to you. Even writing them makes me feel a little uncomfortable. I know personally that many of them provoke a lot of anxiety in me. At the same time, seeing the extremes of our thinking in black and white can also prompt us to a new level of self-awareness and compassion.

As we bring *The Guilt Book* to a close, it is with this idea of a gentle journey in mind. The journey out of false guilt can be a slow and challenging one. Whilst you might have hoped for a very simple equation to make it all go away, we have shown you that false guilt lies at the very heart of our views about ourselves. Try not to let the magnitude of the problem make you feel overwhelmed. At this stage of the journey, you are equipped with eight key supports:

1. An understanding of the difference between true and false guilt.

2. A perfect model to resolve all true guilt.
3. An understanding of how the mind works in relation to guilt.
4. An awareness of cultural and social influences on developing false guilt.
5. An ability to spot common pitfalls in resolving false guilt.
6. A set of hard tools to attack false-guilt problems.
7. An understanding of how to accept Jesus' forgiveness for true sin.
8. A 'bill of rights' to remind you of how you can live each day.

Reducing the impact of false or lingering guilt on your life will not just correct your theology. Working on this aspect of your thinking will have profound benefits for your confidence, self-esteem, sense of joy and your relationship with God and others.

Surrender to proceed

Much of what you have read within *The Guilt Book* has related to abandonment, surrender, acceptance and realization. All of these acts seem passive and counter-intuitive; however, in the scheme of this piece of work they are all essential if you are to make a recovery.

Surrender at this juncture means simply to concede that your previous attempts to get rid of false guilt have failed. As a result, you are giving up your old 'map' for a new one that promises a much better destination. To help you do this, simply sit quietly and meditate on the lyrics of 'White Flag' by Chris Tomlin:

The battle rages on
As storm and tempest roar

We cannot win this fight
Inside our rebel hearts
We're laying down our weapons now

We raise our white flag
We surrender
All to you
All to you

We raise our white flag
The war is over
Love has come
Your love has won

Here on this holy ground
You made a way for peace
Laying your body down
You took our rightful place
This freedom song is marching on[8]

Surrender for power

It would be easy to believe that surrender disables us from participating in a battle. Instead, the surrender we are encouraging here empowers you to fight the *right* battles, that is, against false guilt, not against yourself. By giving up some of the self-defeating battles you have been engaging in, you can actually apply your full capacity to those that are beneficial for you to fight.

In the battle with false guilt, there is a need for careful discernment, since our feelings are frequently misleading. Using them instinctively will very often lead you to begin applying the wrong techniques to the wrong issues. If you feel compelled to resist a thought or to examine a memory, be suspicious about whether it is the right battle. Pray for God's discernment whenever you feel false guilt attacking you or provoking you into action. You will need to pick which battles to fight – ask for his help in choosing.

Surrender to love

I recently found myself, coincidentally, arm modelling for my dear friend, artist Charlie Mackesy, whilst he created a new version of his well-known sculpture, *The Prodigal Son*. As I stood still and attempted to hold the pose of the Father's arm, I was struck by the incredible limpness Charlie had expressed in the Son's frame. It was an embrace of complete surrender and one of absolute love.

The Prodigal Son, Charlie Mackesy. Used with permission.

Like the prodigal, many of us have kept our guilt in mind, filled with worries about how we could ever now live in our Father's house, and how we can make ourselves acceptable. He, on the other hand, has got different plans for us, plans to hold, love and remake us. Our best work is simply to melt into those all-powerful arms and let him do his work. Brennan Manning says,

> Absolutely nothing can separate us from the love of Christ. Neither the imposter nor the Pharisee, neither the lack of awareness, not the lack of passion, neither the negative judgements of others nor the debased perception of ourselves, neither our scandalous past nor our uncertain future, neither the power struggles in the church nor the tensions in our marriage, nor fear, guilt, shame, self-hatred, nor even death can tear us away from the love of God, made visible in Jesus the Lord.[9]

Surrender for others

The best thing about surrendering is that it redeems and restores things you were trying to do before. Things that used to be slaves to guilt can now be used for God's glory.

1. From compulsive caring, you can now become a genuine carer – able to love within helpful boundaries and give selflessly.
2. From thinking others better than you, you can now genuinely think the best of others, with no need to compare, contrast and compete.
3. From being ashamed of who you are, you can now shout with St Paul, 'I am not ashamed of the gospel' (Romans 1:16), and boast of the cross of Christ and what this means (Galatians 6:14).

At the start of this book, we shared the idea that people who struggle with guilt are trying to escape from a prison cell. Well, there is nothing worse than escaping from the cell but then trying to walk through life with the jailer's ball and chain still attached. This large lump of metal will damage anything nearby.

This is a life's work, of course – a journey in every sense of the word – and we will continue to get this wrong until we go to heaven. But we believe that surrender is the key thing that will enable you to leave behind the ball and chain as well as the prison cell. This is surely an important step.

The haven of peace revisited

In the introduction, we shared the idea of a haven – or safe harbour – that would mark the end of your journey to freedom from guilt. We used a quote from Charles Spurgeon:

> Great thoughts of your sin alone will drive you to despair;
> but great thoughts of Christ will pilot you into the *haven of peace*.[10]

You will have worked out from reading this book that thoughts of sin and thoughts of Christ are likely to co-exist as long as you are on this earth, but we want to ask a simple question: 'What is the prevailing wind?'

Before you started reading this book, we imagine that the thoughts of sin were much the stronger, blowing you away from the shore. We hope and pray that, as you come towards the end of this book, this wind has lessened and you have been able to benefit more from thoughts of Christ.

Are you now in a position where you can 'enjoy'[11] thoughts of Christ, such that they might fill your sails and blow you towards this 'haven of peace'? There will be gusts in the other direction, because you will keep making mistakes, and life events will continue to occur. These gusts will help you to repent of true guilt and evaluate the false.

But has the *prevailing* wind changed? Are you now heading 'home'? If so, you have broken free from guilt, even if peace is still at some distance. These thoughts are driving you towards the haven of peace, and the closer you get, the better you will feel.

The best news of all, of course, is that these thoughts (as well as filling your sails) will actually pilot you *into* the haven. God is the best journeyman of all and he stands beside you on the deck as you sail home.

Summary

As you courageously continue the journey of gentle surrender over the coming weeks and months, Rob and I pray that you will not only find a great increase in your sense of joy, but that you may know more of the unconditional love and grace that God has for you and begin to enjoy him all the more. We pray that these realities, beyond everything else, will bring healing and transformation into your life.

Exercises

At the start of the book, we encouraged you to take a 'mug-shot' of yourself as you began your journey with guilt. Repeat this now, and spend some time thinking about where you stand with guilt *after* reading this book:

- What is the first thing that springs into your mind when you hear the word 'guilt'?

  _____

  _____

  _____

- How far does the expression: 'Looking good, feeling bad' reflect your circumstances?

  _____

  _____

  _____

- What one thing is different, having read the book?

  _____

  _____

  _____

- What one thing do you want to change next?

  _____

  _____

  _____

Here are a few other review questions from this chapter, but chiefly we want you to concentrate on the exercise above.

⇨ Were you aware that false guilt is turning aggression inwards, to hate the self? Were you aware that there was an opposite position – but not one of hating others? How would you define this 'opposite position'?

⇨ What did it feel like to write a 'bill of rights'?

⇨ How 'attached' to your guilt are you? Are you attached to any other negative things in your life?

⇨ How does it feel to abandon abandonment and kill the impostor spirit – does this feel like loss or gain? Why?

⇨ What did you learn from the 'White Flag' song by Chris Tomlin?

⇨ What thoughts came into your mind when looking at *The Prodigal Son* sculpture?

Some possible answers to the 'I' statement revision exercise

(from p. 159)

I deserve punishment . . .
Low self-esteem and experience of parental guilt induction can leave people believing that everyone deserves forgiveness apart from them. False guilt becomes a means both of remembering why they deserve punishment as well as being a punishment in and of itself.

I feel bad, so I must have done something wrong . . .
Many people suffer from intrusive and unwarranted guilt feelings, particularly when they are under stress. Overvaluing these feelings leads people to seek out the 'reason' for them and subsequently remember things to feel bad about.

I need to be certain . . .
A large proportion of those who suffer from disabling guilty feelings have perfectionist tendencies and struggle with the fact that they have made mistakes. They tend to ruminate or stew on their errors, trying to work out just how bad they really are. The result isn't that they now feel better; they typically feel worse and less certain about what they actually did.

I need to be safe . . .
Some people use guilt as a mechanism that, they believe, will keep them from making future mistakes. Their refusal to release their sins to memory keeps them in a state of perpetual anxiety, always on the lookout for the opportunity to 'go wrong'. As a result, their guilt is constantly being activated and reviewed.

I am always to blame . . .
Those who come from critical family settings can absorb the idea that they are more responsible for mistakes than they really are. As a result, any issues or conflicts become 'their fault'. Very often these individuals will make quick apologies and avoid upsetting people at any cost. Their intolerance of guilt is overcome simply by accepting it immediately.

I don't deserve success . . .
Some of those who struggle with false guilt simply don't believe that they are worthy of any success. This is often described as 'impostor syndrome'; with greater success/responsibility come increasingly guilty feelings. Guilt becomes an expression of the anxiety that a person feels when the professional perception of them and their own low self-image grow increasingly apart.

Appendix 1: Prayers and meditations

The discernment prayer (when exploring the difference between true and false guilt)

Lord Jesus Christ,

Through the power of your Holy Spirit, give me the discernment to separate those things for which I should feel appropriately guilty and those where my guilt is misplaced. You are all truth, and I pray that you would cut through the confusion and distortions of my human conscience, even if it be too blunt or too acute. Give me the strength to face those things that are hard to see and the courage to keep looking at them from beyond my discomfort.

In all of this, affirm your love for me and your desire to see me fully embrace the freedom that you have offered to me through your death and resurrection life.

In your holy name,
Amen.

The sinner's prayer (when conscious of true and unrepented of sin)

Dear Father God,

I have recognized my true guilt for the things that I have done, thought and said that have offended you, for things that have hurt my neighbour and damaged myself. I have tried to run and hide from the reality of these things, but I cannot carry the burden any longer. Today, I acknowledge my sin, I recognize your authority over me and I accept that the punishment I deserve was laid upon your Son Jesus Christ for my sake. I receive the forgiveness that you offer me now and I invite your Holy Spirit to dwell in my heart. Remove my guilt, as you have promised, and fill me with grace and thankfulness.

In Jesus' name,
Amen.

The walk (a meditation on the prison cell)

(Read this story though three times and invite the Holy Spirit to speak to you through it)

You are sitting on a thin mattress, looking towards a small window to your right. The late afternoon light is streaming through the window and warming your face. You imagine what it would be like to be standing in an open field, with the warm sun touching your body, feeling light and free.

Suddenly, you turn your eyes back towards the walls around you. They are cold and bland, marked by scrawled graffiti. As you look closely, you see that every scratched phrase is an accusation against you. Everything you have ever done wrong is written on the walls. Some words stand out: 'Failure', 'Disgusting',

'Shameful', 'Unlovable', 'Guilty'. Your stomach churns, and your hands go cold as you realize what is weighed against you. You sense that you will never be worthy enough to stand in the sun.

You look to your left and you see that the door of your cell remains open. It has been like this for many months, indeed, since your sentence was completed. And yet you cannot leave; the accusations on the walls keep you a prisoner. This place of separation feels right. It reminds you of your failures; it keeps your guilt alive. Punishment is your only solace.

You hear a voice from outside the door. It is clear and warm: 'Come to me, my child. Your sins are forgiven. I love you.' Your heart lifts, and you stagger to your feet. Yet, as you stand, the words on the walls seem larger and more powerful. They oppose you, and you collapse on the stone floor. As you look, you see the man at the door. He steps into the room, wiping his flat hands over the cold stone.

Behind every move of his hand is a trail of blood. It smears over every accusation, over every sin, over every mistake. You look on, powerless to stand. The man stops and crouches in front of you. He smiles a warm and knowing smile. As he extends his hands to you, you reach up and steady yourself against him. He senses you looking back at the walls, but he urges you on; there is nothing to see here.

Now, you find yourself in the field outside the window. You stand, arms outstretched in the late afternoon sun. You feel peace. You feel forgiven. You feel free.

A prayer of forgiveness for guilt induction

Dear Jesus,

I recognize that my emotions have been influenced by those with
the responsibility for my care and that their use of guilt has been
partially responsible for my current pain. Regardless of whether
their influence on me was intentional or accidental, I release to
you my anger and disappointment about their actions. I choose
to forgive them and pray that you would fill my heart with
feelings of forgiveness.

I now pray that you might heal the influence of guilt
induction on my life. I refuse to submit to the manipulation of
my conscience by others; instead, I ask that you would give me
the courage to stand in the authority I have as a son / daughter
of God.

In Jesus' name,
Amen.

A prayer for courage to challenge false guilt

Lord Jesus Christ,

I have become bound by feelings of false guilt. These feelings
relate both to actual sins that I have been forgiven for and to
events or thoughts over which I have had absolutely no
influence or control. These feelings of guilt are stealing
my ability to live in the light of your salvation. They have
robbed me of my peace and have kept me from the service
of others.

I ask you to strengthen my resolve to fight for my peace
by using the tools that have been outlined to me. In your
strength, I choose not to repeat my prayers for forgiveness,

nor to confess my mistakes repeatedly, but to work on
the faulty processes in my mind that keep these feelings
alive.

I trust in your grace and compassion towards me in this
difficult battle.

Thank you, Jesus, that you are victorious over all things.

Amen.

The compassion prayer (for times of self-criticism and self-attack)

Lord God,

You created me and you know me.

You have made me in your image and have loved me with an
everlasting love.

When I have turned my back on you, you have turned your
face towards me.

When I have stumbled to the floor, you have restored my
dignity.

When I have been full of criticism, you have been full of
compassion for me.

As I am tempted to agree with the enemy's accusations
against me, let me hear your voice of love.

I put the weapon-words I would use against myself down
before you.

I pick up your words of acceptance, comfort, love and
patience.

I choose to treat myself as you treat me and as my neighbour
would wish to be treated.

In Jesus' name,
Amen.

The abandonment prayer (for when you need to give up fighting your fears)

Lord Jesus,

I abandon myself to you.
I abandon control of my past to the cross.
I abandon control of my future to your plans.
I abandon the fear of man, for your acceptance of me.
I abandon my guilt and shame, for your forgiveness and love.
I abandon my self-hatred, for your deep compassion.
I abandon running away, for sitting in the ashes.
I am not abandoned.
I am found in you.

Thank you, Jesus.
Amen.

Appendix 2: More practical help

The next few pages contain some extra material that will help you go deeper in a few areas. They are not essential, but may help answer some questions you have along the way, and will direct those of you who need it to further resources and help.

Contents

1. What is the Cognitive Behavioural approach?

Cognitive Behavioural Therapy, or CBT, was first clearly outlined by an American psychiatrist and psychoanalyst called

Aaron T. Beck, whom we met earlier. As a psychoanalyst, he spent a lot of his time trying to interpret and discover his patient's unconscious defence mechanisms and anxieties. However, it occurred to him one day that it might be easier actually to ask the person what thoughts were in his head. This is not to say that psychoanalysis is no good – it is very good for some types of problems – but for many common mental health problems, CBT has been found to be the most effective form of therapy and the one most often recommended by the NHS. At its core is asking about thoughts: what went through your mind; what did you think next; how does this thought relate to this other different thought, and so on. CBT never asks the *why* question, although you often end up realizing why yourself!

As well as thoughts, it looks at behaviours, especially avoidant behaviours, and times when you have escaped from a situation. CBT therapists are also interested in the more subtle 'safety' behaviours that allow you to keep on going in an anxious situation, but never fully help – something that actually makes the problem worse in the long term.

The idea is that, by changing unhelpful thoughts and modifying unhelpful and cyclical behaviours, you will be able to help the person's mood. This typically takes around twelve sessions – two or three for helping the person to understand their problem, two or three to get more evidence about how to change, between three and six for changing, two or three for making sure things are really fixed and so that you know what you need to keep on doing in the future. Some simple phobias will be quicker; some more complex anxieties and ruminations can take up to thirty sessions. The sessions are typically weekly or fortnightly and an hour long.

To find out more about CBT and locate a local accredited therapist, visit www.babcp.com.

2. What to do when guilt really takes hold

Self-help books like this one can be really helpful – especially if you read them alongside a friend or relative who can help you think through what they are asking and help you stay on track. However, they are the *most simple* level of intervention. There will be some people who need more help with their guilt – and this might include seeing a GP, seeing a therapist (preferably a CBT therapist), and even seeing a psychiatrist and taking medication if you are clinically depressed. It is unlikely that simple guilt would result in you needing to go into hospital, but sometimes the ensuing depression can be so severe that this is advisable.

All of this sounds a bit scary, which is why this section contains resources to help you find the right person to talk to. Remember, all of these people do these jobs because they want to help those who struggle with their mental health, and they may even have had such problems themselves. However, if you are cautious, it is absolutely fine for you to take someone along for the consultation and explain that you would like them to sit in, at least for the beginning. As a psychiatrist, I (Rob) know how grateful I am when people bring someone along to the consultation, as it lets me know that the person has support and also that they are more likely to remember what I say!

3. Seeing a therapist

If this book really resonates with you and you think you need more help, we would recommend that you see your GP and ask them to refer you on. We would also say that you are better off seeing a secular therapist who is good rather than a Christian therapist who is not so good. Maybe you can find a good Christian one, though sometimes it is helpful to see someone who does not share your faith, as you really have to examine many of your assumptions, which may unwittingly have been keeping the problems going.

We would recommend seeing a Cognitive Behavioural Therapist if you have ongoing and chronic guilt or seem to be totally out of touch with any guilt. A number of other types of therapy can help in this area, and these include person-centred therapy or psychodynamic therapy. However, it is CBT that has the most research-based evidence for effectively treating depression, and this is the basis for this book. The national association of accredited CBT therapists, all of whom have trained to post-graduate diploma level, is the British Association of Behavioural and Cognitive Psycho-therapists. You can find out more at www.babcp.com and follow the links to www.cbtregisteruk.com, or by calling BABCP on 0161 705 4304.

4. Getting urgent help

There are times when you need to talk to someone *now*. The list below gives you the relevant telephone numbers.

NHS Direct (England and Wales)	24-hour advice for people in England and Wales Call the new non-emergency number of 111, or in some areas it is still 0845 4567 www.nhs24.com
NHS 24 (for Scotland)	24-hour advice for people in Scotland 0845 242424 www.nhs24.com

Lifeline (for Northern Ireland)	If you are feeling suicidal 0808 808 8000
Your local A&E/ Casualty/ER	These are open 24 hours a day, and you can just walk in if it is a genuine emergency. Remember, not all hospitals have an A&E department. Look for the red sign.
Call 999	In a real emergency when you cannot get to the hospital, you can call 999 from any phone and ask for an ambulance.
The Samaritans	A confidential phoneline you can call if you are feeling suicidal 0845 909090 www.samaritans.org jo@samaritans.org

5. More about depression

Psychiatrists use sets of symptoms to diagnose mental illnesses, as there are typically no lab tests that can be done as in some other specialities. A common definition is from the ICD-10[1] and says,

> In typical mild, moderate, or severe depressive episodes, the patient suffers from lowering of mood, reduction of energy, and decrease in activity. Capacity for enjoyment, interest, and concentration is reduced, and marked tiredness after even minimum effort is common.
>
> Sleep is usually disturbed and appetite diminished. Self-esteem and self-confidence are almost always reduced and, even in the

mild form, some ideas of guilt or worthlessness are often present. The lowered mood varies little from day to day, is unresponsive to circumstances and may be accompanied by so-called 'somatic' symptoms, such as loss of interest and pleasurable feelings, waking in the morning several hours before the usual time, depression worst in the morning, marked psychomotor retardation, agitation, loss of appetite, weight loss, and loss of libido.

Depending upon the number and severity of the symptoms, a depressive episode may be specified as mild, moderate or severe.

You shouldn't worry too much about whether you can identify with everything in this description. Instead, ask yourself, 'Does this describe me fairly well?' There are fact sheets available on depression that can tell you more, or which you can give to friends, employers and relatives to explain what is going on – see the Royal College of Psychiatrists' website.[2]

On the internet, you will easily find copies of things called the Beck Depression Inventory, the Hospital Anxiety and Depression Scale and the PHQ-7. These are self-rating scales for depression and will give you an idea of whether or not you are depressed. However, please remember that these are only screening tools, and it will be your GP who will be able to tell you how bad your depression actually is.

Your ability to use a self-help book like this will vary depending on how depressed you are. We think you will find it interesting at any level, but for people who are more severely depressed, we would want to be cautious about how much it will change things and maybe suggest that you read it with a friend.

Severity of depression	Not depressed, but struggle with occasional guilt	Mild depression, where your predominant problem is guilt	Moderate depression that is starting to affect your everyday functioning	Severe depression that significantly handicaps you
How to use this book	This book may explain some of your feelings and help you understand some Bible passages that you have found hard until now.	This book is really designed for people like you to work through and make a major difference to how you think and feel.	This book will be useful, but you will need some help – maybe from a friend or relative who can read it with you, or possibly from a professional via your GP.	This book will not help that much with the severity of your guilt. (You will need professional help.) But it may help you understand some things and how your faith fits in.

6. What about more severe guilt and depression?

Not looking after yourself

People who really struggle with guilt can become depressed and believe that they are not worth looking after, or that to deprive their body of nutrition is an appropriate punishment for how bad they have been.

If at all possible, please keep eating – even if all you can do is keep a basic diet going with plain foods. Consider supplementing this with vitamin tablets if your diet is very poor. If you lose more than a stone (or 10kg) or drop more than two dress sizes (or lose more than four inches from your waist) or are losing weight rapidly (more than 1kg or 2lb per week), please see your GP urgently.

Please also be aware that rapid re-feeding or binge eating after a long period of near-starvation can be damaging for your body, and you should see your GP before doing this.

Suicidal ideas or plans

When your mood is really low and your thinking is really negative, wanting to get away from it all is a very natural feeling. For some people, this can extend even to wanting to harm themselves or end their own life. If this is you, please see your GP or call for help as soon as possible!

Some things to remember if you are feeling like this:

- It's OK to talk about it – this does *not* make you more likely to do something; in fact, it can be a relief.
- Help *is* available, both from the NHS and your local church. See the emergency numbers a few pages back.
- People will *not* be better off without you – this is the depression telling you a lie.

- These thoughts are not sinful – they are part of an illness and not your fault.

Debt and financial worries

When you are very low, you can sometimes fail to pay attention to everyday matters like paying bills or checking your cashflow. You may also be less able to deal with debt logically when you are not thinking too clearly. Fortunately, there are a number of organizations who want to help you at such times. Please see one of the free national resources below rather than going to a loan company.

- Christians Against Poverty – www.capuk.com (01274 760720)
- Community Money Advice (run by Christians) – www.communitymoneyadvice.com (01743 341929/ 790909)
- Citizens Advice Bureau (local government) – www.citizensadvice.org.uk (local phone numbers)

Martin Lewis (Money Saving Expert) has also developed an excellent free 'debt and mental health' advice pack that Rob contributed too. Download from www.moneysavingexpert. com/credit-cards/mental-health-guide.

OCD and guilt

Obsessive-compulsive disorder (OCD) is a mental-health issue in which an individual has obsessive thoughts and compulsive behaviour (which can be more thoughts). An obsession is an unpleasant thought, image, question or doubt that repeatedly enters a person's mind, causing them high anxiety. The compulsion is an attempt to remove or resolve that obsession. It could be an act like washing your hands, but for many

OCD sufferers it is a mental process like rumination, mental checking, praying or repeating words. The OCD cycle usually has four stages:

1. Obsession – a violent thought enters your mind (e.g. stabbing your friend).
2. Anxiety – you feel terribly anxious and wonder what sort of person would have this thought.
3. Compulsion – you ask yourself questions about why you had the thought. You research articles about murderers on the internet to see if you are like them. You avoid your friend just to be on the safe side.
4. Temporary relief – you feel better, but it doesn't last, and soon doubts and fears return.

OCD has three key emotional components:

Doubt + Anxiety + Guilt

Everyone who suffers from OCD experiences powerful false guilt, although they are often convinced that they are horrible people who fully deserve to feel terrible guilt. Compulsive confession is commonly seen in OCD as a means of escaping the powerful guilt and anxiety that a suffer feels. However, no amount of confession and reassurance is enough to resolve the dilemma.

If you think you might be suffering from OCD, it is essential to get professional help, as your condition will not go away on its own. Three of the best places to start are:

- www.ocdaction.org.uk
- www.ocduk.org
- www.ocdonline.com

7. What to do if you start slipping backwards

Over the next few months, we hope that you will continue to grow more and more in how you manage guilt and how you enjoy life. However, as you will have gathered by now, this journey is unlikely to be totally smooth. There are going to be some bumps and wiggles along the way.

How we react when a setback comes along can make all the difference – if we are able to roll with the punches a bit, this can mean that we ride over these setbacks. If, however, we panic and overreact and predict that this will result in a disaster, this can turn the setback into a genuine disaster, and we can be back at square one.

The following list is something you should read if you are having a bit of a bumpy ride. We hope it will keep your thinking on track and mean that the bump will only be a bump and not a disaster. Take the time to make some notes about what you feel about each tip.

	Practical tip	Your notes
1	You know that setbacks are likely to occur. This was likely to happen at some point.	
2	Setbacks are temporary, and short-term hiccups will usually settle after a few days.	
3	Setbacks do not mean disasters or that you are back to square one.	
4	A setback can be a positive experience, allowing you to build on the skills you have learnt.	

	Practical tip	Your notes
5	Setbacks can be predicted – identify some situations where they might occur.	
6	Do not avoid whatever caused the setback – this needs to be dealt with.	
7	Do not escape from the situation by leaving or drinking alcohol – it *will* settle.	
8	You have learned a range of skills during your reading of this book – use them now or read through your notes.	
9	Set yourself targets to get back on track – start off with some short-term ones to get to tomorrow.	
10	If you have tried all of the above, talk to someone who will be able to give you good advice. Who will you talk to?	

Keep a note here of situations where you might be likely to have a setback:

⇨ _____

_____

Keep a note here of what you did when you met a setback and what happened:

⇨ _____

_____

Appendix 3: More resources

Time to change

We are passionate about ending the stigma against mental-health problems within the church. This situation is not made any easier by spiritual healing ministries which claim to have got mental health all figured out.

The church has come a long way in the last 2,000 years in overcoming stigma on many issues – Jew and Gentile, black and white, rich and poor – but the whole area of health and healing is still controversial. Physical illness (such as cancer or a broken leg) is better understood, but mental illness is often still seen as a sign of weakness or deficient faith.

We believe, along with many others who work with people with mental illnesses, that it is 'time to change'. This is the title of a major government campaign to end stigma – www.time-to-change.org.uk. You might like to visit the website and read/watch some of the stories and testimonies.

We also believe that this is not fundamentally an issue of theology, but an issue of education. It has been education that has helped overcome stigma in every debate: Gentiles are worth saving too; black people are fully human; the rich and the poor will be in God's kingdom. It is education that will win the day here too, and our prayers for a church that understands mental distress and does not try to hide it or 'theologize' it away.

Frank's story

Well-known heavyweight boxer Frank Bruno brought this degree of ignorance to light when he was detained under the Mental Health Act in 2003 because of a manic episode. *The Sun* newspaper ran the headline: 'Bonkers Bruno locked up'.[1]

Second editions of the paper responded to the massive public outcry, re-phrasing it as 'Sad Bruno in mental health home'. Today, Frank and his daughter Rachel are advocates for 'Time to Change'.[2]

You might read the above story and cringe, but similar abuses based on ignorance take place every day. People who are denied jobs because of mental illness, people who are teased because they 'need antidepressants', people who have to move house because they are mocked for being the 'local nutter'.

It would be unhelpful and wrong for us to label this as either true guilt (for there is no guilt here) or false guilt (for these people are not making this up). Instead, it should be called what it is – destructive stigma based on ignorance. It is indeed time to change.

LLTTF with God

The Mind and Soul Foundation teamed up with an international company called Five Areas to produce a resource called 'Living Life to the Full with God'.

This is based on the popular Living Life to the Full website (www.llttf.com) which has over 2 million users in the UK, but adds a Christian perspective and also gives you access to additional modules for free.

The course offers online help for anxiety and depression, using a number of modules with audio, video and eBooks. You can access this through the Mind and Soul Foundation's website at:

www.mindandsoulfoundation.org

You can also order a course pack (about £120 including training) and run this course as an evening class in your church. It is suitable for either a Christian or non-Christian audience – you can decide how much faith-based content to put in.

Other books on depression and guilt

Chris Williams, Paul Richards and Ingrid Whitton, *I'm Not Supposed to Feel Like This: A Christian Approach to Depression and Anxiety* (Hodder & Stoughton, 2002). ISBN: 978–0340786390. www.fiveareas.com.

The classic Christian book on depression and anxiety from a CBT point of view. Easy-to-use techniques supported by relevant Christian illustrations. This book will be a great help if you struggle with significant levels of depression as well as guilt – for example, if you have become self-isolated, have reduced activity or struggle to do anything.

Paul Tournier, *Guilt and Grace* (Hodder & Stoughton, 1962). ISBN: 978–0340009642. Second-hand only.

No-one has written a Christian book on guilt from a psychological perspective since this one – over fifty years ago. Now well out of print, second-hand copies, however, can be found online. Based on a psychoanalytic approach to guilt and quite heavy, it is still full of wisdom and help.

John Lockley, *A Practical Workbook for the Depressed Christian* (Authentic, 2002). ISBN: 978–1860242267.

Guilt is not all about depression, but it is a big part of it. This hefty book covers everything you need to know about depression, its psychological and biological causes and treatments (including medication) – all with a helpful Christian commentary. Chapter 22 is about guilt.

Windy Dryden, *Overcoming Guilt* (Sheldon, 1994). ISBN: 978–0859696869. Very cheap second-hand.

This is not a specifically Christian book, but is sympathetically written. One of the first books in the popular 'Overcoming' series, this slim book is packed full of practical wisdom and experience in counselling people who struggle with guilt. Based on CBT techniques. Dr Dryden has written over 120 books, many on self-help.

Join other readers online

You can read this book with others by joining our online forums and chat, as well as discover additional material on guilt by visiting:

www.mindandsoulfoundation.org

You will find articles, testimonies and talks on guilt, as well as all the other resources of the Mind and Soul Foundation's website.

About the Mind and Soul Foundation

The Mind and Soul Foundation is a national networking, equipping and encouraging organization for people who are interested in how Christianity and mental health problems relate.

We have three main aims – to link up people across the UK who are interested in Christianity and mental health, to put together high-quality resources for the church on this topic, and to share information about what is already going on near you. Some of our resources are:

- major annual conferences with high-quality speakers and seminars
- databases of Christian counsellors, mental health projects and mental health-friendly churches across the UK
- over 400 articles on a wide range of topics, with polls, forums and comments

- regular emails highlighting new resources
- audio and video archive of over 150 talks.

www.mindandsoulfoundation.org

Notes

Introduction

1. A presentation of the Christian gospel called 'Two Ways to Live' can be found at www.matthiasmedia.com.au/2wtl. It is simple, even simplistic, but it illustrates the core truths – and the things false guilt can rob us of.
2. P. Tournier, *Guilt and Grace: A Psychological Study* (Hodder & Stoughton, 1962), p. 213.
3. Enid Blyton, *The Folk of the Faraway Tree* (Hamlyn Young Books, 1976), p. 120.
4. For a summary and Christian perspective on this film, see the review on the Damaris website (www.damaris.org/content/content.php?type=1&id=190).
5. C. H. Spurgeon, *Morning and Evening: Daily Readings* (1896), now published by Alban Books Ltd, Edinburgh. Reflection from the evening of 27 March.

1. Guilty or not guilty – two types of guilt

1. Paul Tournier, *Guilt and Grace: A Psychological Study* (Hodder & Stoughton, 1962), p. 213.

2. NIV 2011.

3. Psychopathy is something we could talk about much more. Some people have stated that society is becoming more psychopathic – that we are doing things we would not have considered thirty years ago (read more at http://chronicle.com/article/The-Psychopath-Makeover/135160). Conversely, the increasing influence of bodies like the United Nations and democratic governments is cited as evidence that we are becoming 'nicer' (read more at www.psychologytoday.com/blog/wired-success/201302/are-we-becoming-nicer). Our view is simply that mankind has always needed, and will always need, God – but the ways in which, and degrees to which, we fall short may differ.

4. For a detailed discussion of many such issues, see John Stott, *Issues Facing Christians Today*, 4th edn (Zondervan, 2006).

5. Attributed to Richard Challoner, *Considerations upon Christian Truths and Christian Duties* (J. P. Coughlan, 1826).

6. Have you noticed that people who struggle with guilt seem to have an almost perfect memory of every conversation they have ever had? The question we want to ask is: 'Is it worth the brain space, given the stress it causes as they constantly review them?'

7. In quoting 1 Peter 1:16, we might not notice that it follows a section offering a 'living hope' (verse 3) and one that will never 'perish, spoil or fade' (verse 4). Our pursuit of holiness has become death to us, and the guilty stain of perceived sin has arrived. Instead, it is clear that our inheritance is 'kept in heaven' and our faith 'shielded by God's power' (verses 4–5).

8. King Cnut (or Canute) was a king of England and Denmark who lived c. 995–1035. He wanted to show his court that he was merely a man, and that God was the only one with true power. So he positioned his throne in the face of the incoming tide and promptly got wet!

9. A charity called SOBS (Survivors of Bereavement by Suicide: www.uk-sobs.org.uk) provides local and phone support, as well as reviewing lots of relevant resources.

10. Those who wish to know more about this might like to read about psychoanalysis and the Freudian theory of guilt, but be warned, it is quite heavy going.

11. R. Janoff-Bulman, *Shattered Assumptions: Towards a New Psychology of Trauma* (Free Press, 2002).

12. Some people are not good with numbers. They prefer letters A→E or emoticons from smiley face to sad face or a scale they have made up themselves. The important thing is that you know what it means.

2. Guilty as sin – and how true guilt is healed

1. J. C. Ryle, *Warnings to the Churches* (Banner of Truth, 2007), p. 106.

2. An example is the story of Ananias and Sapphira (Acts 5:1–10) who covered up some rather crucial financial details.

3. For a profound illustration of what it means to be adopted into God's family, read 'Father's Love Letter' (a paraphrased compilation of Bible verses) – a popular internet resource (www.fathersloveletter.com).

4. Guido Rocha was a Brazilian sculptor who was tortured for political activism. His statue of Jesus in extreme pain on the cross was on display at the fifth World Council of Churches assembly in Nairobi. However, it was removed as it caused quite a lot of offence. Judge for yourself, and see the image at www.twentytwowords.com/2010/05/16/the-tortured-christ.

5. This is based on the many 'Confessions' that can be found throughout the various liturgies of the world.

6. If you are into history, this great little book covers it all. K. Birkett, *The Essence of the Reformation*, 2nd edn (Matthias Media, 2009).

7. M. Luther, *Galatians*, Crossway Classic Commentaries (37–38) (Crossway, 1998).

8. Professor Herant Katchadourian, 'Guilt as Social Control', Stanford University (http://alumni.stanford.edu/get/page/magazine/article/?article_id=29708).

9. Brown University, 'Legitimization under Constantine', (www.pbs.org/wgbh/pages/frontline/shows/religion/why/legitimization.html).

10. The Second Vatican Council of 1962–65 reviewed a number of Roman Catholic beliefs, but was also marked by a genuine grace and spirit of negotiation. It focused on the relationship of the Catholic Church to the modern world. Read more at http://en.wikipedia.org/wiki/Second_Vatican_Council.

11. For a longer discussion on whether morality can arise from outside of religious traditions and divine revelation, see http://en.wikipedia.org/wiki/Secular_morality.

12. W. Golding, *Lord of the Flies* (Faber and Faber, 1954).

3. Guilty by design – why false guilt flourishes

1. This 'Initiative vs. Guilt' is the third (preschool) stage of psychoanalyst Erik Erickson's 'Psychosocial Development'. Read more at http://en.wikipedia.org/wiki/Erikson's_stages_of_psychosocial_development.

2. We will come back to the emotion of shame in chapter 7.

3. Budding psychologists might have noticed here that moral development is not usually seen as part of Erikson's 'Psychosocial Development', and is more usually attributed to a psychologist called Lawrence Kholberg. Read more at http://en.wikipedia.org/wiki/Lawrence_Kohlberg's_stages_of_moral_development. However, please forgive us this as we try to give readers a short overview of the development of guilt.

4. Sigmund Freud, *The Interpretation of Dreams* (London: Wordsworth, 1987). For more about the Analytical School, see http://en.wikipedia.org/wiki/Psychoanalysis.

5. A 'behaviourist' in this context is someone who purely studies the behaviour of their experimental subjects and not what they are thinking or why. Ivan Pavlov and his famous salivating dogs is an early example of this type of research.

6. U. Wagner et al., 'Guilt-Specific Processing in the Prefrontal Cortex', *Cerebral Cortex*, November 2011, 21: 2461–2470.

7. Daniel G. Amen, *Change Your Brain, Change Your Life: The Breakthrough Program for Conquering Anxiety, Depression, Obsessiveness, Anger, and Impulsiveness* (Piaktus, 2010).

8. For some helpful leaflets about depression and the feelings that can result, see the website of the Royal College of Psychiatrists: www.rcpsych.ac.uk/expertadvice/problemsdisorders/depression.aspx.

9. T. R. Cohen, S. T. Wolf, A. T. Panter and C. A. Insko, 'Introducing the GASP Scale: A New Measure of Guilt and Shame Proneness', *Journal of Personality and Social Psychology* 2011, 100 (5): 947–966.

10. T. Brooks (1652), *Precious Remedies against Satan's Devices* (CreateSpace Independent Publishing Platform, 2012).

11. The fact that things get more complex as we get older is a normal experience. If we understand this, it will help a lot. For a simple overview of the 'stages' our faith will progress through, see http://en.wikipedia.org/wiki/Fowler's_stages_of_faith_development. It is normal to question, to need to be less black and white, to stand back – this will result in time in a deeper faith and trust. For an audio seminar on this by Rob Waller, listen to www.htb.org.uk/media/stayin-alive.

12. Roger Ellis, *The Occult and You* (Authentic Media, 2004).

13. C. Williams, *Overcoming Depression and Low Mood: A Five Areas Approach*, 4th edn (Taylor Francis, 2013). Visit www.llttf4.com. Reproduced with permission.

4. Guilt edged – a life tinged with badness

1. See www.beliefnet.com/Health/Emotional-Health/ Christians-Take-Depression-Seriously.aspx.

2. See www.selfhelpformums.com/get_over_motherhood_guilt.

3. Visit www.psychologytoday.com/blog/healthy-connections/ 201109/are-you-guilty-parent.

4. www.familyanatomy.com/2011/03/10/depressed-parents-why-their-kids-feel-bad-too/.

5. K. Aunola, A. Tolvanen, J. Viljaranta and J. E. Nurmi, 'Psychological Control in Daily Parent-Child Interactions Increases Children's Negative Emotions', *Journal of Family Psychology* (2013).

6. Aaron Rakow et al., 'The Relation of Parental Guilt Induction to Child Internalizing Problems When a Caregiver Has a History of Depression', www.ncbi.nlm.nih.gov/pmc/ articles/PMC2808109/ (accessed 20/1/2014).

7. Carl Gustav Jung, *Four Archetypes* (Routledge, 2003).

8. The psychiatrist and psychotherapist Henry Rey (1912–2000) used this idea to describe how some patients can become attached to psychiatric hospitals, which he termed 'Brick Mothers'. The containing walls of the asylum can never replace the arms of a truly loving mother, and the bricks are harsh and scratchy. The pervasive emotion felt is guilt, and whether the 'child' can do more to draw out love. You can read more about this and see some cartoons here: www.rcpsych.ac.uk/discoverpsychiatry/studentassociates/ perspectivesonpsychiatry/drawingfromlife/keepingmum.aspx.

9. There is some debate over the difference between shame- and guilt-based cultures, e.g. you could say the bad feelings that relate to exclusion are more aligned to shame, being slightly different from the guilt experienced through damaging the environment by driving a thirsty motorbike. However, for the sake of simplicity and because the treatment responses to both false guilt and shame are so similar, Rob and I are inviting you to see the bigger picture and avoid imposing a strong distinction between the two.

10. With apologies to our overseas readers. You put in here the different types of motorcycle and style in your country . . .

5. A guilty conscience – spotting false-guilt traps

1. Paul Gilbert, *Overcoming Depression: A Self-Help Guide Using Cognitive Behavioural Techniques* (Robinson, 1993), p. 251.

2. Arthur C. Zepp, *Conscience Alone Not a Safe Guide* (Christian Witness Company, 1913), p. 103. Sourced from David A. Seamands, *Healing for Damaged Emotions* (Victor Books, 1981), p. 78.

3. Wikipedia entry for Rumination: http://en.wikipedia.org/wiki/Rumination_(psychology).

4. Joachim Stoeber and Julian H. Childs (2010), 'The Assessment of Self-Oriented and Socially Prescribed Perfectionism: Subscales Make a Difference', *Journal of Personality Assessment* 92 (6): 577–585.

5. Liberate Conference, York 2013, run by Mercy Ministries UK (www.mercyministries.co.uk).

6. 'Guilt Beyond a Reasonable Doubt': www.ocdonline.com/articlephillipson2.php.

7. Anne Wilson Schaef, *Meditations for Women Who Do Too Much* (HarperCollins, 2013).

8. R. Shafran, S. Egan and T. Wade, *Overcoming Perfectionism* (Robinson, 2010).

9. The UBC Word for Today, 'Jesus, Your Mediator', 17 March 2014, www.ucb.co.uk/word-for-today-23504.html.

6. Guilt and shame – facing feelings and actions

1. François-Marie Arouet Voltaire, *Zadig, ou la Destinée* (*Zadig, or the Book of Fate*) (1742), published in French (Hachette, 2004).

2. Mark Freeston is Professor of Clinical Psychology at the University of Newcastle. His website can be found at www.ncl.ac.uk/psychology/staff/profile/mark.freeston, and his dragon-slayer story can be downloaded as a PDF from the website of the charity OCD UK: http://tinyurl.com/krzs6dx.

3. These are described in J. K. Rowling, *Harry Potter and the Goblet of Fire* (Bloomsbury, 2000).

4. Tony Gough, *Don't Blame Me: How to Stop Blaming Yourself and Other People* (Sheldon Press, 1990).

5. See ch. 6 in Will van der Hart and Rob Waller, *The Worry Book* (IVP, 2011). Find more information about uncertainty at www.mindandsoul.info/worry.

6. Extract from van der Hart and Waller, *The Worry Book*, p. 117.

7. Adapted (with permission) from a collection of similar behavioural experiments that counsellors may wish to look into more deeply, but are probably too advanced and technical for the average reader. J. Bennett-Levy et al., *Oxford Guide to Behavioural Experiments in Cognitive Therapy* (OUP, 2004).

7. Accepting forgiveness – living in the present

1. P. Tillich, *The Courage to Be* (Yale University Press, 1952), p. 152.

2. For a detailed psychoanalytical look at guilt and shame, and also how to address them in therapy, see A. Clark, 'Working with Guilt and Shame', *Advances in Psychiatric Treatment* 2012, 18: 137–143.

3. Paul Gilbert, *Overcoming Depression: A Self-Help Guide Using Cognitive Behavioural Techniques* (Robinson, 1993), p. 235.

4. Heinz Kohut, *The Analysis of the Self: A Systematic Approach to the Psychoanalytic Treatment of Narcissistic Personaltiy Disorders* (International Universities Press, 1971).

5. Paul Tournier, *Guilt and Grace* (Hodder & Stoughton, 1962), pp. 189–190.

6. *Les Misérables* is a showcase for the two ways to respond to God: in grace or by works. For a website dedicated to understanding how we can learn about God through this book/film, see www.damaris.org/lesmis.

7. This quote is from an unknown source, but has been attributed to Ceylonese priest Daniel Thambyrajah Niles (1908–1970).

8. Brennan Manning, *The Ragamuffin Gospel: Good News for the Bedraggled, Beat-Up, and Burnt out* (Multnomah, 1990).

9. Matt Redman and Jonas Myrin, 'You Alone Can Rescue', © 2009 Thankyou Music/Said and Done Music.

10. Dr Fred Luskin, *Forgive for Good* (HarperOne, 2003).

11. Ibid., p. 34.

12. Ibid., p. 194.

13. J. Lockley, *A Practical Handbook for the Depressed Christian* (Authentic Media, 1991), p. 304.

14. The idea of a 'safe place' has been much ridiculed in Hollywood films, but try it – it might even work.

15. These techniques are based very loosely on the idea of Compassionate Mind Training, first outlined in ch. 10 of P. Gilbert, *Compassion: Conceptualisations, Research and Use in Psychotherapy* (Routledge, 2005). They are taken further in the work of Shaun Lambert on a Christian model for mindfulness in S. Lambert, *A Book of Sparks: A Study in Christian MindFullness* (Instant Apostle, 2012). Help on how to find a good therapist is given in Appendix 2.

16. Paul Gilbert, *The Compassionate Mind* (Constable, 2010), p. 233.

17. Tournier, *Guilt and Grace*, p. 112. In this book, Paul Tournier makes many comparisons between the role of the therapist in loving the patient and how God loves us even as sinners. Does the therapist get paid for the session? To be sure! But the therapist has also chosen this as their career and lifelong calling.

8. Guilt and joy – a better journey

1. David Seamands, *Healing for Damaged Emotions* (Victor Books, 1981), p. 49.
2. For a more detailed discussion of the pop psychology of self-esteem and the lies we have been sold, see G. Harrison, *The Big Ego Trip: Finding True Significance in a Culture Of Self-Esteem* (IVP, 2013).
3. Terry D. Cooper, *Sin, Pride & Self-Acceptance: The Problem of Identity in Theology and Psychology* (IVP Academic, 2003), p. 163.
4. Malcom France, *The Paradox of Guilt: A Christian Study of the Relief of Self-Hatred* (Hodder & Stoughton, 1967), p. 106.
5. Please note, we are not talking about an actual spirit like a demon. This is just a figure of speech, and no deliverance is needed.
6. See Acts 9:1–4.
7. William H. Shannon (ed.), *The Hidden Ground of Love: The Letters of Thomas Merton on Religious Experience and Social Concerns* (Farrar, Strauss, Giroux, 1985), p. 146.
8. Chris Tomlin, Jason Ingram, Matt Maher and Matt Redman, 'White Flag', © 2013.
9. Brennan Manning, *Abba's Child: The Cry of the Heart for Intimate Belonging* (NavPress, 1994), p. 156.
10. C. H. Spurgeon, *Morning and Evening* (1896), now published by Alban Books Ltd, Edinburgh. Reflection from the evening of 27 March.

11. Some Christians struggle with the idea that God is to be
     'enjoyed'. Instead, they associate God more with words such
     as 'worth' and 'awe'. However, the leading American
     Conservative evangelical, John Piper, has called us to
     'Christian hedonism' – not to enjoy the sins of the world,
     but the love of God. Read more about this term at http://
     en.wikipedia.org/wiki/Christian_hedonism. Piper got into a
     bunch of trouble over this, but people have come to see that
     he is right – when we desire God himself (not his forgiveness,
     his power or his heaven – but him himself!), we discover the
     good news of the gospel. The gospel, Piper argues, is not
     about God but *is* God. When we are forgiven, we get freedom,
     to be sure, but we also get God – in relationships, as family, to
     walk with – or maybe even sail with!

Appendix 2: More practical help

1. 'International Classification of Diseases': version 10. The full
   link is http://apps.who.int/classifications/icd10 and then
   search for 'depression'. Text reproduced with permission.
2. The full link is www.rcpsych.ac.uk/expertadvice/
   problemsdisorders/depression.aspx.

Appendix 3: More resources

1. www.theguardian.com/media/2003/sep/23/
   pressandpublishing.mentalhealth.
2. www.time-to-change.org.uk/news-media/celebrity-
   supporters/frank-bruno.sw.